Political Campaigns

By Peter Kogler

T0002709

Cavendish
Square

New York

Published in 2021 by Cavendish Square Publishing, LLC
243 5th Avenue, Suite 136, New York, NY 10016

Website: cavendishsq.com

This publication represents the opinions and views of the author based on his or her personal experience, knowledge, and research. The information in this book serves as a general guide only. The author and publisher have used their best efforts in preparing this book and disclaim liability rising directly or indirectly from the use and application of this book.

All websites were available and accurate when this book was sent to press.

Library of Congress Cataloging-in-Publication Data

Names: Kogler, Peter, author.
Title: Political campaigns / Peter Kogler.
Description: New York : Cavendish Square Publishing, 2021. | Series: Topics today | Includes bibliographical references and index.
Identifiers: LCCN 2020003330 (print) | LCCN 2020003331 (ebook) | ISBN 9781502657480 (library binding) | ISBN 9781502657473 (paperback) | ISBN 9781502657497 (ebook)
Subjects: LCSH: Presidents–United States–Election–Juvenile literature. | Presidents–United States–Nomination–Juvenile literature. | Presidential candidates–United States–Juvenile literature. | Political campaigns–United States–Juvenile literature.
Classification: LCC JK528 .K64 2021 (print) | LCC JK528 (ebook) | DDC 324.973–dc23
LC record available at https://lccn.loc.gov/2020003330
LC ebook record available at https://lccn.loc.gov/2020003331

Editor: Jennifer Lombardo
Copy Editor: Michelle Denton
Designer: Deanna Paternostro

Some of the images in this book illustrate individuals who are models. The depictions do not imply actual situations or events.

CPSIA compliance information: Batch #CS20CSQ: For further information contact Cavendish Square Publishing LLC, New York, New York, at 1-877-980-4450.

Printed in China

Find us on

CONTENTS

THE LONG ROAD TO ELECTION DAY

In the United States, the day people vote for the next president falls on the first Tuesday after November 1 every four years. Voting for members of Congress is held on this day every two years. The importance of Election Day cannot be understated, as voters take to the polls to determine which politicians will be allowed to lead the country, as well as their state and local community.

Election Day is only possible because of the countless people and tireless efforts involved in the long road of campaigning that it takes to get there. Volunteers, potential voters, campaign staff, and even financial donors all have a part to play in the political campaigns that influence election results. While Election Day is largely a democratic process, it's not always a perfect system. Currently, the ability to vote on Election Day is open to Americans of all races, genders, and backgrounds who are legally registered to vote. This has not always been the case, though. When the country was established, only white American men who owned land were allowed to vote. Years of reforms have led to constitutional amendments that have opened the door to millions of voters.

The demographic of voters isn't the only thing that's changed, nor is it the only thing that continues to change. For example, the road to Election Day is becoming an increasingly expensive one. A 2014 article from *TIME* magazine stated, "Since

◀ Politicians run campaigns to convince people to vote for them.

Women had to fight hard to gain their right to vote. This photo shows women campaigning for that right.

the mid-1980s, the amount dumped on elections by campaigns and outside groups, as measured by the Federal Election Commission (FEC), has grown 555 percent—faster than even the alarming increases in the costs of health care and private college tuition."[1] The costs are expected to keep growing in future elections. However, some studies have found that despite the increase in campaign spending, voter turnout has decreased in some elections.

The Changing Campaign Landscape

Election advertising is where a lot of the campaign money goes. Before the invention of television, politicians relied mainly on newspapers and personally touring cities across the country to reach out to voters. Today, however, there are more advertising options than ever before. The increased use of social media websites such as Twitter, Facebook, and YouTube, as well as news apps and targeted ads on other websites, has increasingly allowed for a higher level of engagement with voters.

The downside of this increased access to voters is that now anyone can spread misinformation in an effort to discredit other candidates and their campaigns. These efforts are known as "influence campaigns," and the ease of creating fake profiles on social media has allowed them to become more common in recent years. Some people believe social media websites have a responsibility to police and take down profiles that appear to be fake. In 2018, CBS News wrote, "Large internet firms are taking active steps to remove content and accounts associated with influence campaigns. Twitter, a haven for bots and trolls during the 2016 presidential campaign, recently removed 770 accounts associated with Iranian and Russian influence campaigns. It said the accounts were 'sharing divisive social commentary' and images."[2]

The process of campaigning continues to evolve and change with each new advance in technology or law that aims to protect the election process. Numerous guidelines and regulations are in place to ensure the transparency and fairness of the system, but corruption and fraud are still very real problems on the campaign trail. The cost and effort it takes to run a successful campaign are increasing. The results on Election Day show whether or not the work and money that went into the campaign were actually worth it.

The Ultimate Decision

American voters throughout history have helped make decisions that have had major effects on events around the world as well as in their own country. The politicians they vote into office and the political parties those politicians represent have the power to start and end wars, fight for human rights, and make other decisions that change the quality of life around the world and the environment in which people live—for better or for worse.

PRESIDENTIAL ELECTIONS FROM START TO FINISH

Presidential campaigns are the most expensive and, some argue, most historically important political races in America. Whoever wins the presidency becomes the most visible leader of the country for at least four years. Presidential candidates don't just appear out of nowhere; they're the faces of the political parties they represent, and they've worked their way up to that point through a series of nominations and wins, competing against others within their own party. Eventually, however, only one candidate from each party is left standing to compete for the presidency.

The road to the White House typically follows the same cycle every four years, and it's a lengthy one. By the spring of the year before a presidential election is held, candidates who wish to run for president should have announced their intentions to do so. For example, someone who wanted to run for president in 2020 would typically have to announce their candidacy by the spring of 2019. A series of debates begins in the summer, allowing candidates to answer questions about their policies so voters can see where they stand on certain issues and make an informed decision on Election Day. From January or February to June in the year of a presidential election, voters in each state select which candidate they would like their political party to nominate for

◀ Getting into the White House requires years of strategy, hard work, and fundraising.

president. In the summer or early fall, each political party holds a national convention in which one candidate is officially nominated to run for the presidency. From there, the long road to Election Day continues. In November, after months of campaigning, rallies, televised debates, and more, people vote for their next president. However, even after Election Day officially takes place, more work is yet to come.

In December, the Electoral College receives its votes from electors; Congress counts these electoral votes in early January and officially declares the winner of the presidency. The winner is called the president-elect until they are officially sworn in as president. While the process may seem long and complicated, it's important for voters to have a basic understanding of how the election process works.

An Early Start

In December 2018, the first candidates for the 2020 presidential election began setting their campaigns—in their earliest forms—into motion. Even though the election was more than 670 days away at that point, these potential candidates knew the importance of getting a head start. Candidates need time to gather everything they'll need to last through the whole campaign, such as large amounts of money and campaign managers to oversee the entire process. The idea of a campaign is to sway people to the candidate's side, and voters also need time to look through all the information and make a choice they're happy with. There's no specific time when a candidate needs to announce their intentions to run, but recent campaigns seem to be getting earlier starts.

In 2018, the *New York Times* reported, "In 1960, John F. Kennedy did not announce his candidacy until 11 months before Election Day. As recently as the 1992 election, Bill Clinton did not formally enter the presidential contest until just over a year before the general election. But since then, campaigns have grown longer, bloating into nearly two-year affairs."[1] Research has shown that candidates who get a late start struggle more; they have difficulty raising enough money and getting organized

The opposite of a campaign announcement is called a Shermanesque statement, in which a candidate declares that they absolutely will not run for office. This comes from the American Civil War leader General William Tecumseh Sherman (*shown here*), who stated multiple times that he would never run for president and would never serve even if he won.

in time for the earliest round of voting. By deciding to look into joining the race very early on, candidates give themselves more time to get a feel for the political landscape in front of them. This can be accomplished by forming exploratory committees, which help them determine if there would be enough support for their campaign before they officially commit to the race.

Under the regulations set forth by the FEC, creating a presidential exploratory committee allows individuals to raise and spend up to $5,000 before having to officially register as candidates. Using these guidelines, potential candidates can gauge voter support by running polls and traveling within their district and state to meet potential voters. Some individuals may find that they don't have enough voter support to win the election. If this is the case, they generally don't bother registering as a candidate so they can save their time and money.

It's important that the committee doesn't raise more than the $5,000 limit, make any official statements, or advertise publicly during its exploratory campaign. If the committee breaks any of the strict guidelines set by the FEC, the individual will need to officially register as a candidate. Some plan to do this anyway—if their exploratory committee has found that voter, financial, and political support will be enough to run a strong campaign. Once they register, more than $5,000 can be raised and spent.

Even if an exploratory committee finds that support for a candidate is strong, there's no guarantee that the candidate will win. The next step for those who enter the race is to win their party nomination; if this doesn't happen, their journey ends there. There are winners and losers all the way up to Election Day.

Caucuses and Primaries

According to the Council on Foreign Relations, "The presidential nominating process in the United States is one of the most complex, lengthy, and expensive in the world."[2] To decide which candidate will be nominated, political parties hold two different kinds of votes in different states: state primary elections and caucuses. Although they're not the same thing, both kinds of votes

The Earliest Election Days

Election Day has always been in November, but not always on the first Tuesday. In the late 1700s and early 1800s, each state was allowed to decide when it would hold Election Day, as long as it was within the 34 days before the first Wednesday in December. At the time, most people in the United States worked as farmers, so November was chosen as the election month because it was the best time for them; the season for farming was over in November, and winter wouldn't have hit too hard yet. Voting before it started to snow was important because, in the days before mass transportation, most white landowning males (who were the only ones allowed to vote at the time) needed several days to travel to their polling places, and bad weather conditions would make this difficult—sometimes impossible.

Eventually, technology in communication and transportation improved greatly—and different Election Days suddenly didn't seem too smart. People started to worry that some states' elections could be influenced by the outcome of elections in other states; for example, if Illinois voted two weeks ahead of Iowa, voters in Iowa might use the outcome of the Illinois elections to decide who they were going to vote for. This could change the outcome of the entire election, and many people felt it was unfair. Some people were also concerned that voters would travel to another state and vote again. In 1845, Congress made Election Day the first Tuesday after November 1 for every state. Tuesday made sense at the time because even with faster transportation, it still took a day or two for many people to travel from their farms to their voting location. Voters would often leave after church on Sunday. Today, however, many people work on Tuesdays. Most states require employers to give employees time off to vote, but about 20 states don't, so some people—especially those who work more than one job—don't have time to vote. The polls are generally open until late at night, but the lines are often long. For these reasons, there's a push for the law to change Election Day to a weekend or to make that Tuesday a national holiday so no one has to go to work.

What Is the FEC?

The Federal Election Commission (FEC) was created by an amendment to the Federal Election Campaign Act (FECA), which was passed in 1972. This act was long overdue; presidents had been calling for better legislation since 1905. FECA set rules about where campaign money could come from and how much each candidate could accept.

After reports of campaign finance violations in 1972, Congress strengthened FECA in 1974. It also created the FEC—an independent government organization—to enforce the regulations and to make sure candidates were honest about reporting their fundraising. The FEC began operating in 1975, and several other campaign finance reform laws have been passed since then, such as the Bipartisan Campaign Reform Act of 2002. However, many people believe there's more work to be done to make presidential campaigns fairer for all candidates.

have the same goal of nominating a potential presidential candidate. The two major political parties, Democrats and Republicans, each hold primaries and caucuses. Caucuses have a longer history in presidential elections than primaries, but they're also less popular in modern elections. As of 2020, only 14 states, the District of Columbia, and four US territories use caucuses.

Caucuses are party-sponsored events. First, local assemblies are held, and representatives of each candidate give speeches to persuade others to vote for their candidate. At the end of the event, the number of votes for each candidate is tallied. These votes determine the number of delegates won for each candidate. These delegates, in turn, go to a county or state convention and vote for delegates who will represent each candidate at the party's national convention later that year. This number varies by state.

A primary is a general vote. Registered members of a party go to their polling place, just like they do on Election Day. They cast their vote for the person they want to be president.

In a direct primary, that candidate wins that state. In an indirect primary, just as with a caucus, the number of votes determines the number of delegates a candidate gets. However, unlike a caucus, these delegates don't choose other delegates; they simply go on to the national convention themselves to cast their vote for their candidate.

There are multiple different types of caucuses and primaries,

Presidential candidates, such as Bernie Sanders (*shown here*), are treated as celebrities. Many people want to meet and take photos with the candidate they support.

The two main political parties are the Democrat and Republican Parties, but others exist too. Two "third parties" can be seen on this ballot from the 2016 US presidential election.

and they vary from state to state. For example, one common type is called a closed system. This means you have to be a registered member of a party to vote. Someone who's registered as an independent—meaning they're registered to vote but don't belong to any political party—or as a member of one of the smaller political parties, such as the Green Party, can't vote in closed Republican or Democratic primaries or caucuses. The other types of primary and caucus are:

- open: anyone can vote for any candidate, no matter what party they belong to
- semi-closed: voters must either be registered members of the party they're voting for or independent; for instance, in a semi-closed Republican primary, only Republicans and independents can vote for the Republican candidate
- semi-open: anyone can vote regardless of how they're registered, but they have to choose a party when they get to their polling place

There's also variation in how the delegates are awarded to the candidates. Many Republican primaries operate on a winner-take-all basis. This means the candidate who gets the most votes gets all of the delegates available. Democratic primaries are more likely to use a system called proportional representation. This means that any candidate who gets at least 15 percent of the votes in a caucus or primary gets at least one delegate. Every delegate a candidate wins votes for them at the Democratic National Convention (DNC). These are called pledged delegates because they've committed to voting for that candidate. Unpledged delegates, also called superdelegates, don't have to commit before the DNC and are not selected based on voting in primaries or caucuses. They can change their mind about who they're voting for at any time, right up until the final vote is taken. The use of superdelegates has been controversial because some people think it's unfair.

Despite the more widespread use of primaries, caucuses still have their place on the road to the presidency. The Iowa caucuses are especially famous and receive a lot of press coverage that can really help a candidate, as the publicity leads to stronger party unity and higher financial donations that could help them win the campaign.

After the caucuses and primaries are over, the awarded delegates make their way to the DNC and Republican National Convention (RNC).

National Conventions

National conventions are generally held in the summer of a presidential election year. They're intended to get both major political parties to rally behind the candidates they want to win. Experts say these events are about bringing the party together to support their candidate rather than allowing the candidate to talk about the policies they would put into place if they won. Conventions are intended to boost morale, get delegates and party members excited, and get as much press as possible. These are highly televised events that occur over the course of four days, during which delegates that were awarded during the caucuses and primaries cast their votes. The location of these conventions changes every election cycle; host cities are generally chosen for the number of people they can accommodate as well as the quality of hotels and the variety of entertainment in the area. Many cities hope to be chosen to host these conventions because of the economic boost that comes with them.

On the first day of both conventions, a prominent party member typically gives a speech called the keynote address. In an article for ThoughtCo., US government and history expert Robert Longley wrote, "Almost without exception, the keynote speaker will emphasize the accomplishments of his or her party, while listing and harshly criticizing the shortcomings of the other party and its candidates."[3] During the second day, a group called the Credential Committee works to confirm that the delegates from the caucuses and primaries are who they say they are. This prevents anyone who isn't an official delegate from sneaking in and casting a vote that could change the outcome of the nomination. The party also announces its platform to convention attendees on the second day. A platform is made up of all the policies the party intends to put into place if its candidate wins the presidency. Platforms are carefully crafted in an effort to appeal to both loyal party voters and people who haven't yet decided which candidate they're voting for. Because the president needs the support of members of their party in Congress to get laws passed, the party must be in general agreement about the platform. This is why a majority (more than half) of delegates must approve the final platform in a public vote at the convention.

On day three, the delegates begin the nominating process. Each state has a delegate chairman, or a person who's been chosen to speak for all the delegates of that state. The chairman gives a speech nominating a candidate, and at least one other delegate from that state gives their own speech backing up the nomination. This process continues for every state.

Once all the candidates have been nominated, the final votes take place. Delegates from each state announce the total number of votes they're casting for a candidate. To win the party's nomination, a candidate must get a majority of votes. If no single candidate gets more than half the votes after the first time around, the delegates will give more speeches and then vote again. However, because of the way the primary and caucus system has been designed, as of early 2020, neither party has required more than one vote since 1952.

The candidate who wins has often already announced the name of their running mate—the person who will be their vice president if they win—several days or weeks prior. In the past, the people at the convention would choose their presidential candidate's running mate; the candidate had no say in it. This was the tradition until 1940, when Franklin D. Roosevelt became the first and only president to win a third term. At that point, Roosevelt decided to replace John Nance Garner, who had been the vice president for the previous two terms, with Henry A. Wallace, a man he trusted more. Ever since then, it's been traditional for the presidential candidate to choose their own

There is generally a celebration at the national convention after the winning candidate is officially announced.

running mate based on a number of factors, including how well the two work together, how popular the running mate is likely to be with voters, and how much political experience the running mate has.

On the fourth and final day of the national convention, the delegates go through the same process of nominating the vice president as they did for the presidential candidate. Although they no longer need to do this because the method of appointing a running mate has changed, they follow the tradition anyway. During the convention, the presidential and vice presidential candidates give acceptance speeches, and the candidates who didn't receive the nomination often give speeches encouraging the rest of the party to support the nominees.

These conventions are full of formalities, traditions, and a certain amount of symbolic show, such as the nomination of the vice president. It's a very precise and calculated way of showing the world the kind of power, money, and commitment these political parties have.

Onward and Upward

After the national conventions, campaigning takes on an even higher importance, as the presidential candidate needs to secure the voters and the funding to run a successful presidential race. Swaying people to their side is important long before Election Day; if a candidate is seen as someone who would make a good president, then they'll have a much easier time raising funds to run campaign ads and travel around the country to appeal to new voters. The ability to fundraise tends to create a positive cycle: Candidates who can raise a lot of money tend to be seen as having a better chance of winning, which sometimes causes

Political campaigns set up headquarters in multiple states. Shown here is Eric Trump—son of US president Donald Trump—at the 2016 Trump campaign's New Hampshire headquarters, calling voters to ask them to vote for his father.

more voters to join their side and donate. In contrast, those who have trouble fundraising from the beginning are likely to have even more difficulty later on because people tend not to want to donate to the campaign of someone who's likely to lose the race.

People who strongly support the candidate can volunteer to work on their campaign. One important job volunteers do is go around their communities and get fellow voters on their side. This can be done by putting up signs, handing out fliers, or mailing out informational pamphlets or letters. While the volunteers do the ground-level work, the candidates themselves attempt to connect with potential voters by holding rallies and other events. At these events, the candidate talks about the parts of their platform that the voters in that area have indicated through polls that they feel the most strongly about.

As Election Day nears, both parties step up their media engagement. This includes giving televised interviews and participating in debates, as well as increasing the number of advertisements on television, radio, and social media in a last-ditch effort to win over every possible voter they can. These advertisements, however, do not come cheap. The amount of money a candidate is able to raise often makes the difference between winning and losing in November.

To the Ballot Box

Decades ago, voting was only available to a small subset of the population. The number of people eligible to vote grew slowly. It was nearly a full decade after the country's formation that all white men—not only those who owned land—were given the right to vote. In 1870, black men were legally allowed to vote, but many barriers were put up to prevent them from exercising this right. In 1920, white women—and, technically, black women—were finally allowed to vote. Native Americans and Asian Americans were given the right to vote in 1924 and 1952, respectively, but as with black men and women, unfair laws and occasional violence often prevented them from doing so. It wasn't until 1965, with the passage of the Voting Rights Act, that such tactics were

Exploring the Electoral College

During a presidential election, when American voters cast their ballot, they're actually voting for their state's electors. The number of votes cast by the public is called the popular vote, but the presidential winner is determined by the electoral vote, which is cast through the Electoral College. This is the only American election that takes place indirectly; in fact, the United States is the only democratic country in the world to have this exact system of electing a president.

The Electoral College website explains, "The Electoral College is a process, not a place ... The Electoral College consists of 538 electors. A majority of 270 electoral votes is required to elect the President. Your state's entitled allotment of electors equals the number of members in its Congressional delegation: one for each member in the House of Representatives plus two Senators."[1] Every presidential candidate has a group of electors that has been appointed by their political party. The way these electors are chosen varies by state. If a candidate wins the popular vote in a particular state, they generally also win all of that state's electoral votes. The only exceptions are Nebraska and Maine, which allow electoral votes to be split proportionally among the winners. It's possible for a candidate to win the

made illegal. Voter suppression does continue today, but even though there is more work to be done, voting rights are much more inclusive now than they were when the country was founded.

All states require voters to be registered, but the cutoff date for registration is different in each state. Some states require voters to be registered weeks in advance, while others allow people to register when they show up to vote. Some voters don't even need to be present to vote; they can fill out and mail what are known as absentee ballots for Election Day. The laws for absentee voting, like most other voting laws, vary by state, but they typically cover voters who are ill, disabled, away at college, on vacation, serving in the military overseas, or who have no popular vote but lose the electoral vote; however, this has only happened five times in history as of early 2020.

After Election Day, the chosen electors meet in their own states. The electors use separate ballots to vote for the president and vice president. These votes are recorded on what's called a "Certificate of Vote." The certificates are then sent to Congress to be tallied on January 6 by House and Senate members. Whoever wins the majority wins the presidency.

The Electoral College has been the subject of much controversy in recent years. Some people say the United States should get rid of it because it's unnecessarily complicated, outdated, and unfair. Others think we should do what the Founding Fathers wanted. These people also often say that no democratic system is perfect and we shouldn't get rid of our system just because it has problems. The Founding Fathers created the Electoral College for several reasons. One was that they wanted to make voting fairer among the states; they wanted small states to have an equal say even though they had fewer people. Another was because some of them didn't trust voters to make an informed choice.

1. "What Is the Electoral College?," US National Archives and Records Administration, December 23, 2019, www.archives.gov/federal-register/electoral-college/about.html.

transportation to the polling place. Absentee ballots are restricted only to voters who cannot physically be at the polls.

For those who will be at the polling place on Election Day, the process can take anywhere from a few minutes to several hours, depending on how long they have to wait in line. Voters first check in with volunteers at the polling place to confirm their identity. Then, they enter a private booth to complete either a paper ballot or an electronic one, although paper ballots are later also electronically scanned and stored. Once the polls close, the secured ballot boxes are taken to a central counting office.

The county board of elections uses a variety of methods to tally the votes and report the numbers to their state's office. Most places use computers today. The website LiveScience explained that most of the machines in polling places have a memory card in them that's collected and transported to the counting office along with a printed record of the number of votes. The memory cards are put into a computer, which "tallies all of the results and begins to generate a preliminary vote-count report."[4] Absentee ballots are also tallied and reported at this time. The preliminary vote count is then relayed to state officials and the press. There are various ways of doing this. According to LiveScience, "In some places, a 'stringer' for the Associated Press (AP) will sit there and call in the results to the central AP call center ... In other places, the results will be pushed via phone or internet to state officials, who will report the results."[5]

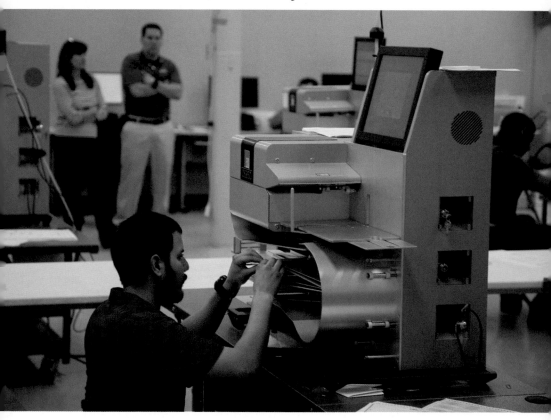

Many places in the United States tally votes with a machine such as this one.

No matter how the votes are counted, there are multiple steps involved to prevent votes from being changed or miscounted. This is why election results can take days or weeks to count, even though fewer than 5 percent of ballots are counted by hand. Within the next couple of weeks, officials in each state meet to verify the election results, then the Electoral College in each state meets to cast their votes. These votes are sent to Congress for a final tally, and a president-elect is officially declared once they win 270 out of 538 electoral votes. The results are continuously announced as they come in, and once a clear winner can be predicted, the loser will often give a speech in which they concede, or admit defeat. This can take place on Election Night or at any time afterward when a loss seems certain. Typically, they thank their campaign members and supporters and congratulate the winner. However, a concession isn't legally binding. In fact, in 2000, candidate Al Gore conceded to George W. Bush, then changed his mind when the votes had to be recounted and it looked like Gore might win after all. He later had to concede again when Bush was announced the official winner.

Inauguration Day

Inauguration Day—the day the new president and vice president are sworn in to office and officially take charge of the country—is held on January 20 (or January 21 if the 20th happens to fall on a Sunday that year). Occasionally, presidents have been inaugurated on other days, but this only happens if the president is taking office after the death or resignation of the sitting president. Many traditions of the Inauguration Day ceremony were set by previous presidents-elect during their own inaugurations. The Joint Congressional Committee on Inaugural Ceremonies (JCCIC) oversees the events of the entire day. Inauguration Day is considered to be a time of great celebration and patriotism for the entire nation, and it officially marks the end of the long road to the White House.

Inauguration Day begins right next to the White House, at a worship service that's traditionally held at St. John's Episcopal Church. The religious aspect of this day dates back to

The amount of media and public interest on Inauguration Day draws huge crowds in Washington, DC. In 2009, Barack Obama's inauguration set a record when an estimated 1.8 million people showed up.

George Washington, who attended a church service after his own swearing-in ceremony. The service was moved to the beginning of the day's proceedings after Franklin D. Roosevelt attended the service before he was sworn in. After the worship service ends, both the president-elect and the vice president-elect, along with their spouses (and possibly other family members) and the Joint Congressional Committee, head to the White House.

At the White House, the outgoing president meets the incoming one, and they travel together to the Capitol Building for the next part of the ceremony. In the past, presidents-elect have made this short journey on foot or in a carriage. Today, the procession is done with a motorcade of bulletproof limousines and a lot of security guards to ensure the safety of all the elected officials. Parts of the military are also traditionally present, as they are symbolically "reviewed" by the incoming president.

The vice president-elect is the first to take their oath of office. Today, this oath occurs in front of the Capitol Building so the public can see it; however, before 1937, it happened privately in the Senate chamber. The oath the vice president-elect takes isn't the same as the oath the president takes, although both oaths involve promising to uphold the Constitution. Once the vice president is sworn in, it's the president-elect's turn.

After the president is sworn in, they give their official inaugural address to the nation in a ceremony that continues on the west terrace of the Capitol Building. In their inaugural

On March 4, 1921, president-elect Warren G. Harding (*backseat, right*) rode in an open convertible to his inauguration, accompanied by outgoing president Woodrow Wilson (*backseat, left*). Today, candidates generally have much more security on their way to the Capitol Building.

address, the new president typically explains their goals for the presidency and their vision of the nation's future. They generally encourage unity and peace throughout the country and with other nations.

A New Leader

After the swearing-in ceremony, the former president and vice president must leave to begin their post-presidential lives. There's no set ceremony for this; some presidents have chosen to have lunch with the former president or attend the inaugural parade with them. Currently, the tradition is for the former president and vice president to be led out of the Capitol by the new president and vice president. On the east front steps of the Capitol, the JCCIC gathers to oversee this event. The new vice president escorts the former vice president and their spouse past a line of military service members, followed by the new president, the former president, and the former First Lady. If the weather is nice, the former president and First Lady leave the Capitol in a helicopter; this tradition was started in 1971 by President Gerald Ford. Lunch is then held in the Capitol Building's Statuary Hall for the new president and vice president.

After lunch, the president and vice president make their way to the White House from the Capitol Building by leading a parade down Pennsylvania Avenue. This parade is full of patriotic floats, motorcades, military regiments, and marching bands. While the president rides in an armored limousine for most of the parade, they can decide to walk part of the parade route if it's deemed safe enough to do so. The length of their walk depends on weather, the presence of political demonstrators, and recommendations by the Secret Service. This is an informal tradition that began in 1977, when President Jimmy Carter walked more than a mile in the parade.

The Presidential Inaugural Committee (PIC) has the final say on which groups will be allowed to march in the parade, and the number of participants is limited to 15,000. As of 2020, only one parade has ever been canceled: the one for Ronald Reagan's

Once the president and vice president have been officially sworn in, thousands of people line the streets to watch the parade head down Pennsylvania Avenue. Shown here are people braving the cold to watch John F. Kennedy's inaugural procession in 1961.

second inauguration in 1985. This was due to dangerously cold temperatures. Once they arrive at the White House, the president, their family, and select guests get to watch the rest of the parade from a reviewing stand.

Let's Have a Ball

Inaugural balls mark the end of the inauguration ceremonies. The first traditional inaugural ball was held in 1809 for President James Madison, and for subsequent presidents, the number of inaugural balls increased in an effort to allow as many people as possible to attend. Hundreds of tickets were sold for the earliest balls, but there weren't many places that could accommodate such a large number of guests. In 1921, President Warren G. Harding asked to get rid of the expensive balls and was given a large private celebration instead.

In 1949, President Harry S. Truman brought the inaugural balls back into style. Today, the PIC oversees the events, and it raises millions of dollars to organize several official balls that are held in numerous locations; the number changes every year, depending on the new president. President Bill Clinton attended 14 balls in 1997, while President Barack Obama had 10 official balls held in his honor for his 2009 inauguration. President Donald Trump attended three official balls the evening of his inauguration in 2017.

Thousands of people attend inaugural balls, such as this one for President Lyndon B. Johnson (*center, dancing with wife Lady Bird*).

The president and First Lady typically only spend a brief amount of time at each ball—just enough to make an appearance before going on to the next one. They also traditionally dance together for one song, which some presidents seem to enjoy more than others. There are also many unofficial balls that are held around the country that night, with tickets ranging anywhere from $75 to $10,000. The official inaugural balls are generally seen as a way to thank the hundreds of political supporters who made the president's campaign a success. It's also the first time the First Lady officially introduces herself to the nation in her new role. Overall, the balls are intended to be a fun reward after long months of intense campaigning.

Your Opinion Matters!

1. Why are there rules about what people can and can't do during presidential campaigns?
2. Why do you think money is such an important part of a campaign?
3. If you were elected president, what changes would you make to the Inauguration Day traditions?

CHAPTER TWO

POLITICAL ADVERTISING IN AMERICA

Today, presidential campaigns—and all campaigns for various political offices—rely heavily on advertising to get their messages out to voters. Campaigns use social media, television, radio, and print to sway voters and create strong public images. While this is certainly the norm for presidential campaigns now, it hasn't always been the case. In 1789, George Washington didn't even receive a nomination. The Virginia Museum of History and Culture explains, "George Washington was held in such high esteem by the other Founding Fathers and was so popular that there were no serious rivals to his election. He did not campaign for the office or give speeches on his own behalf."[1]

However, even though Washington didn't campaign, he also didn't run completely unopposed. There were, in fact, 11 other candidates. At the time, each elector voted for two different people, and the candidate who won the most electoral votes won the presidency. The person who won the second-most votes became the vice president. This system was later changed because there was no guarantee that the president and vice president would share the same views, which meant it would be difficult to get anything done together. In the first American

◀ George Washington was the only president who didn't have to campaign. Shown here is Washington (*front, center*) being sworn in as president by Robert Livingston, chancellor of New York State (*front left, blue coat*). Behind Washington is his vice president, John Adams.

election, Washington won all 69 votes for president from electors. John Adams came in second with 34 votes. Washington and Adams were inaugurated on April 30, 1789, in New York City. This event set traditions that would stick around for generations to come, such as military parades, a church service, and even fireworks displays.

Washington is the only president who never ran a campaign in order to reach the White House. Even when he and Adams were re-elected in 1792, they faced no opposition; in fact, Washington had planned to retire, but after he was asked to serve a second term, he agreed. Again, he received votes from all the electors from each state and was elected president unanimously, and Adams won even more electoral votes than he had the first time.

The First Campaigns

By 1796, however, America had a vastly different political land-scape. Newly formed parties known as the Democratic-Republicans and the Federalists met privately to pick candidates for the upcoming election. These candidates' campaigns mostly consisted of their supporters using newspapers, pamphlets, and face-to-face conversations with people to earn the public's support. That year, Adams won the presidency, but it was a true race this time rather than a unanimous decision.

In the election of 1800, presidential candidates started using political attacks that were intended to damage the public's perception of their competition. These attacks, which used smear campaigns and name-calling to make a point, are still used in today's elections, but several rules have been put in place to try to make them fairer. For example, a candidate can't say anything about their opposition that isn't true, although they can use editing tricks such as dark colors, ominous music, and unflattering photos to try to influence people's opinions of the facts.

Candidates who run for president need a lot of resources if they want to make it to Election Day. These resources include money, political alliances, and political endorsements. An endorsement is when another person visibly throws their support behind a candidate. Celebrities often announce their endorsements for president, as do former presidents. The point of all of these resources is to win votes. Advertising, therefore, is crucial—it allows candidates to become known and recognizable.

The Importance of Print Media

When the first campaigns were being run, print media was the best way to advertise. Candidates could also use word of mouth—getting their supporters to talk about why they would be a good president—but newspaper ads and printed pamphlets were easier to distribute in large quantities, so they were a better way to reach large numbers of voters. Thomas Jefferson used newspapers as a way to get party support in 1800, when he paid the editor of the *Richmond Examiner* to print articles that criticized his opposition and praised his own party. Political magazines were also used to further the opposition between candidates. During the 1884 presidential campaign, political cartoons in partisan magazines, or magazines that supported a particular political party, were published that attacked both Grover Cleveland and James G. Blaine. The images and emotions these cartoons conveyed were designed to leave a lasting impression on American voters. Supporters also made up short songs called jingles to sing or chant to spread word-of-mouth support for one candidate and criticize the other. One example was "Blaine, Blaine, James G. Blaine, continental liar from the state of Maine."[2] This reminded people of scandals that Blaine had allegedly been involved in. In the end, these political cartoons and jingles helped Cleveland win.

Today, print advertisements still exist, but they're less common and are not considered the best way to reach large numbers of voters anymore. However, jingles have stuck around and evolved into a part of advertising that is meant to be just as memorable: the slogan. Slogans are short, one-line messages that are meant to stick with American voters. The creation of slogans is known as sloganeering. Some famous examples of sloganeering include Dwight D. Eisenhower's "I Like Ike" slogan, Barack Obama's "Change We Can Believe In" slogan, and Donald Trump's 2016 and 2020 campaign slogans, "Make America Great Again" and "Keep America Great." These can easily be printed on hats, shirts, and signs—anything the public can see and

In 1884, Blaine's supporters ran political cartoons that made Cleveland look bad for having a child with a woman he wasn't married to. These cartoons damaged his reputation with some voters but weren't enough to cost him the election.

remember. Trump's 2016 slogan was so memorable that its initials, MAGA, are sometimes used to refer to his supporters and their merchandise. People may talk about "the MAGA crowd" or wearing "MAGA hats," which are red baseball caps with the 2016 slogan on them.

Riding the Airwaves

Before television, newspapers and radios were the main ways people got their news, including information about who was running for president. In 1944, Franklin D. Roosevelt even enlisted help from Hollywood to create amusing ads to air on the radio.

By the 1950s, the sale and use of televisions was on the rise.

At this time, most people disliked and mistrusted advertising agencies, seeing them as manipulative. However, Dwight D. Eisenhower, who was running as a Republican against Democratic governor Adlai Stevenson, was persuaded to approach television ads differently. In 1952, he met with a well-known advertising executive to create the first televised presidential campaign ads. According to *TIME* magazine, Eisenhower's "team's media innovation nationalized a celebrity political culture and ushered in the modern candidate-centered campaign."[3]

These brief ads, which ran for no more than 30 seconds at a time, aired at times when television viewership was high. This meant that Eisenhower quickly became more recognizable than Stevenson. This campaign proved to be incredibly effective, as

Dwight D. Eisenhower was the first presidential candidate to embrace television as a campaign tool.

Eisenhower won that year's election by a landslide. Even today, with Americans using the internet regularly, television is still a commonly used tool for presidential candidates. However, these ads don't come cheap. According to PBS, "Political candidates and organizations spend billions of dollars on television ads—by some accounts, as much as 75 percent of a campaign's budget goes directly towards the production and airing of television advertisements."[4]

Today, hundreds of thousands of political ads air on television during presidential campaigns. In 2016 alone, nearly $110 million was collectively spent in campaign advertising during the week

One Minute to the End of the World

On September 7, 1964, a one-minute television ad from the Lyndon B. Johnson campaign forever changed the course of political advertising. The ad was an attack on Johnson's political opponent, Republican Barry Goldwater. It implied that electing Goldwater for president would mean the end of the world. In the ad, a young girl stands in a field as she counts each petal she plucks off a daisy. Her voice is replaced by a man's voice counting down—and his countdown ends with an atomic blast. The American fear of nuclear war was at an all-time high, and most voters were aware that Goldwater had previously made statements—both joking and serious—about bombing other countries. The ad didn't even need to mention his name; everyone knew what it was trying to say, especially when Johnson's disclaimer came up at the end.

The ad only aired once, but it created such a lasting impression that many people still remember it today. It was effective because it played on Americans' emotions, especially their fears. Furthermore, the ad ended up changing the way presidential candidates were "marketed" to the American public. Candidates and marketing executives realized that emotional ads were one key to getting votes. *Smithsonian* magazine explained, "Voters don't oppose a candidate because they dislike his or her policies; they often oppose the policies because they dislike the candidate."[1] Since the Daisy Girl ad aired, political campaigns have made more use of ads that play leading up to Election Day. Political ads are most frequently aired in states where a political party needs the most votes. For example, 2016 Democratic candidate Hillary Clinton focused on airing most of her ads in states that were leaning more toward Trump during the 2016 campaign, such as North Carolina, Florida, and Ohio. In those states, 80 percent of the ads voters saw were from Clinton, and less than 20 percent belonged to Trump. The *New York Times* reported that Clinton did manage to sway some voters in these states with her ads, although they weren't enough to win her the election.

About 70,000 political ads were aired in total during the

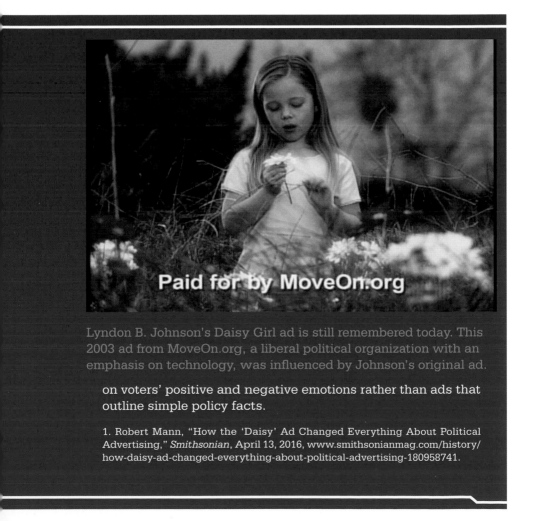

Lyndon B. Johnson's Daisy Girl ad is still remembered today. This 2003 ad from MoveOn.org, a liberal political organization with an emphasis on technology, was influenced by Johnson's original ad.

on voters' positive and negative emotions rather than ads that outline simple policy facts.

1. Robert Mann, "How the 'Daisy' Ad Changed Everything About Political Advertising," *Smithsonian*, April 13, 2016, www.smithsonianmag.com/history/how-daisy-ad-changed-everything-about-political-advertising-180958741.

last week of the 2016 campaign, and nearly all of them—about 92 percent—were negative in tone. This isn't a new trend; negative television ads in campaigns have persisted for years. However, research has shown that negative ads may not improve a candidate's chances more than positive ads. In 2017, the *Journal of Politics* found that although negative ads were more memorable, they may not actually be effective in swaying voters at the polls. The results, however, were inconclusive, as the testing was limited in scope.

At What Cost?

The cost of running any political campaign has risen steadily for decades. Reports from the 2016 Senate elections showed that winning Senate candidates spent an average of $10.4 million, an increase of $1.8 million over the average in 2014. While not every candidate spent that amount of money, some were big spenders. For instance, Senator Pat Toomey of Pennsylvania spent a reported $27.8 million on his 2016 campaign, which was just a fraction of the total cost of the state's 2016 Senate race. Altogether, Pennsylvania spent $164 million, which was made up of both the candidates' campaign spending and outside spending. Since the mid-1980s, *TIME* reported in 2014, spending by campaigns and outside groups on congressional campaigns increased 555 percent.

Presidential elections, too, cost more every four years. In the 2004 presidential election, for example, President George W. Bush and Senator John Kerry both rejected public funding during the primary phase, allowing them to raise collectively almost $1 billion in private financing; then, during the general election, they each received an additional $74.6 million in government funding. More than a decade later, costs rose to a record-breaking high. In 2016, presidential candidate Hillary Clinton spent more than $1 billion in the race to become president. Trump spent slightly more than half that amount, which is closer to what winning candidate Barack Obama spent in 2012. Trump won the electoral vote and the presidency, but Clinton won the popular vote, which almost always wins the electoral vote as well, so it's difficult to tell in this case how much impact the difference in spending had.

Many people are concerned about the increasing cost of campaigning and what effects it might have on the fairness of campaigns. Needing access to such large amounts of money effectively restricts candidates to only those who were already rich to begin with, as candidates spend a lot of their own money on the campaign. This was illustrated in 2019, when Democratic presidential candidate Kamala Harris dropped out of the 2020 race due to lack of funds. Money determines how many voters candidates are able to reach with their message; some people may vote for a candidate simply because they haven't heard much about any of the others. In fact, 94 percent of congressional races are won by the big spenders, regardless of the candidates' qualifications, skills, or voting records. In the era of the internet, it's easier for people to do their own research on each of the candidates than it was in the past, but it's still not a widespread practice.

This emphasis on money has changed the way people run for office. As politician and author Mark Green explained, "Thanks to today's high-cost races, candidates spend very little time running in the traditional sense of the word—mobilizing voters, communicating ideas, debating opponents, attending public

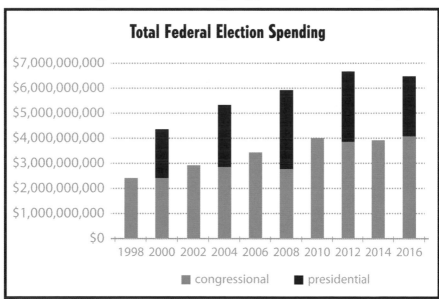

In general, spending on federal elections has been rising, as this information from the Center for Responsive Politics shows.

meetings. Instead, candidates fund-raise for office."[5] Even once they're in office, the fundraising push never ends; they must keep raising money if they want to win reelection and keep their job. Sometimes this impacts their ability to do their job. Critics say this preoccupation with raising money negatively affects politicians' job performance. Too often, these critics say, there's a widespread reluctance by incumbents, or people who are currently in office, to take on controversial issues or issues that are unpopular with major funding sources for fear of losing career-sustaining campaign dollars. In light of legislators' pressing financial priorities, some commentators say it's no wonder that Congress has developed a reputation among voters for doing nothing.

"... And I Approve This Message"

On any political ad, whether it is in print, on television, or on the radio, a disclaimer notice must be attached to it, and there are strict rules as to how the disclaimers are presented. The FEC makes sure candidates follow all these rules. The organization defines a disclaimer notice as "a statement placed on a public communication that identifies the person(s) who paid for the communication and, where applicable, the person(s) who authorized the communication."[6] Within two days after a candidate spends money on anything, including a commercial, they must notify the FEC of how much they spent.

The disclaimer on a political ad falls under one of three categories. Some political ads are paid for by the candidate themselves. Others have messages authorized by the candidate, but the ad itself might be paid for by their party, campaign committee, or another organization that supports the candidate. In these ads, the candidate will say their name and add, "... and I approve this message." The disclaimer will generally say something such as, "Paid for by the Committee to Elect [candidate name]." Sometimes an ad has not been authorized by the candidate, so the candidate will not be featured saying they approve the message. In these cases, the disclaimer will still state who paid for the ad.

The regulations set forth by the FEC control more than just the content of the disclaimer. On printed materials such as newspapers, billboards, and pieces of mail, the notice must appear in a box that is separate from the rest of the ad. The font must be large enough and visible enough to be immediately noticeable and readable. On radio ads that are authorized by the candidate, the disclaimer must be spoken by the candidate. For television ads, if the disclaimer is spoken on-screen by the candidate, they must be in full-screen view. If the disclaimer is done through a voice-over, a clear image of the candidate must accompany it.

Campaigns that use websites, emails, and phone calls to reach voters must also include disclaimer notices. However, campaign items such as pens, stickers, pins, and articles of clothing don't require the disclaimer because they would generally be too small to be readable.

Knowing who has paid for an ad is important information for voters because campaign ads are incredibly biased by design. Positive ads exaggerate a candidate's good qualities, and negative ads exaggerate the opposing candidate's bad qualities. Understanding who wants voters to know this information and why is an important part of being an informed citizen. If an ad paid for by Candidate A says Candidate A voted to increase funding for schools while Candidate B voted to decrease it, the knowledge that it came from Candidate A should make voters aware that they need to look up the facts of each candidates' voting history. Campaign commercials need to tell the truth, but they don't need to tell the entire truth. Sometimes certain facts are withheld that would change the information presented. It's up to voters to do their own research.

Social Media Advertising and Beyond

As the use of social media has exploded around the world, candidates have turned to this new platform for advertising. About 55 percent of Americans report frequently getting their news from social media rather than from the newspaper or television, so it's become a much better way to reach voters. The four main social media platforms that people check for their news are Facebook, YouTube, Twitter, and Instagram.

This truck ad to reelect Donald Trump has a clear disclaimer at the bottom, saying that it was paid for by the Committee to Defend the President. It complies with FEC regulations.

In the past, even when people weren't actively looking for news—for example, while they were watching their favorite show after dinner—political ads could still reach them during commercial breaks, whether they wanted to see them or not. Today, times have changed; a 2017 study from the Pew Research Center found that "six-in-ten of those ages 18 to 29 (61 [percent]) say the primary way they watch television now is with streaming services on the internet, compared with 31 [percent] who say they mostly watch via a cable or satellite subscription and 5 [percent] who mainly watch with a digital antenna."[7] Because most streaming services don't air commercials, putting ads on social media or other websites people visit frequently may be the only way politicians can reach some voters today.

The internet has changed election advertising in ways no one could have predicted. Candidates can now immediately reach millions of potential voters and constantly raise money through online donations. Social media has also allowed for targeted election advertising, which is done by tracking the online footprint of millions of web users. Voters can also try to influence their social media followers by sharing posts.

Some people think this kind of social media engagement makes people more involved in the campaign process and makes it easier for candidates to hear and respond to the issues the public cares about the most. However, others have deep concerns over how much influence social media has gained over our lives and views. One thing people worry about is an advertising tool called microtargeting, which allows every visitor to a specific website to see a different kind of ad based on the views they've previously expressed online and the websites they've visited in the past. The website Recode explained that this process is controversial because many people believe "it permits politicians to target very narrow groups of voters with tailored messages that have the potential to manipulate the political debate."[8]

Another very real concern Americans have is the probability of other countries interfering in US elections. This was proven to have happened during the 2016 election: Russians created fake Facebook and Twitter profiles and spread misinformation on social media that influenced the way people viewed both Hillary Clinton and Donald Trump. Such misinformation is increasingly easy to spread, and even people who are committed to researching things they see online can sometimes be fooled. Microtargeted ads are now seen by some as a threat to democracy because of how easy it is for anyone to create one.

Some people believe it's a website's responsibility to police the ads and posts that people are using to spread misinformation. Some of the moves they've made to improve transparency have been met with approval. For example, as of 2019, Snapchat, Facebook, and Twitter have launched downloadable spreadsheets that keep track of all the political and issue-based ads on their platforms. Snapchat's, for instance, shows things such as who paid for the ad, who it targeted, how much was spent, and how many people saw the ad. Other efforts to police what shows up on their websites have been controversial. For example, in October 2019, Twitter announced that it would no longer allow political ads on the platform. This targets specific candidates, but it leaves open the possibility of buying an ad to inform people about an issue, "which means that while

During the 2016 election, a lot of misinformation circulated on social media. Russian trolls created fake pictures such as this one, which features actor and comedian Aziz Ansari encouraging people to vote through Twitter—even though this doesn't legally count as a vote. By using an image of a famous figure such as Ansari and playing on people's desire for convenience, the Russians hoped to convince Hillary Clinton supporters to stay away from the polls on Election Day.

The Rise of "Dark Advertising"

One of the biggest problems with microtargeting is that it allows candidates to engage in a practice called "dark advertising." This means a candidate can run one ad promising something to one group and a second ad promising the exact opposite to a second group, without either group knowing that the other ad exists. Because the ads change depending on who the computer belongs to or who uses it most frequently, most people will never see an ad that isn't targeted specifically to their group. Unless a candidate announces something out loud, therefore, it's becoming increasingly difficult to know exactly what a political candidate intends to do in office and what they're just promising in online ads to get votes. Experts say this is a danger to democracy because it takes away people's ability to properly discuss issues. When two people never see the same ads, it's difficult for them to agree on whether a candidate represents the country's best interests. Dark advertising can easily be used to trick people into voting for someone who doesn't truly represent their views.

[2020 presidential candidate] Elizabeth Warren can't advertise her bid for the presidency, a political group can still buy ads urging people to vote to protect the environment."[9] Many people believe this move will only restrict political speech while not actually solving the problem of misinformation. Some people also believe it will hurt campaigns that have limited money by making it harder for them to target their most likely supporters without spending millions of dollars.

Other platforms have restricted microtargeting to specific individuals but allow it for more general groups, such as men between the ages of 50 and 60 who live in Los Angeles, California. Critics say this makes it easy for campaigns to get around the restrictions, while supporters of the changes say the fact that the targeting is less precise will make it harder for fake news to be targeted at the people most likely to spread it. One example of this more general

The Mueller Report

On May 17, 2017, former FBI director Robert Mueller was appointed by the Justice Department to look into allegations of Russian interference in the Trump campaign. Mueller was assisted by 19 lawyers, 40 FBI agents, and a team of financial and intelligence analysts. Nearly 3,000 court appearances and 500 witnesses later, Mueller released a 448-page report on April 18, 2019. The report stated Russian interference had indeed occurred through the creation of fake social media accounts. Russian intelligence officers had also hacked email accounts belonging to members of Hillary Clinton's campaign and the Democratic National Committee (DNC).

Mueller had also investigated allegations of financial crimes within the Trump campaign, and he found guilt there as well. Campaign chairman Paul Manafort was charged with money laundering and tax evasion, and several other associates of Trump—many of whom worked on the Trump campaign—were charged with lying to the FBI during the investigation. Mueller reported, "While this report does not conclude that the President committed a crime, it also does not exonerate him."[1] In other words, Mueller didn't come to the conclusion that Trump was fully innocent and that these crimes were done without his knowledge or support, but he also was unable to prove the opposite.

1. Quoted in Erin Dunne, "Mueller Report: Exoneration? Not Even Close," *Washington Examiner*, April 18, 2019, www.washingtonexaminer.com/opinion/mueller-report-exoneration-not-even-close.

kind of microtargeting was a 2016 Trump campaign strategy that used information about people's race and voting history to target black people who didn't vote frequently. These people saw ads that showed Clinton saying racist things about young black men. This was "a voter suppression effort aimed at getting those voters to stay home, and limiting microtargeting would make such an effort more difficult to execute in such a precise way."[10]

Some people believe the issue of microtargeting is overstated and that platforms are using it to draw attention away from the problem of people sharing fake news in the form of memes and unresearched articles. These cost no money at all to upload and share, so they can reach many more people and influence the outcome of an election. Some have pointed to Donald Trump's frequent use of Twitter as an example. Experts have proven many of the things he says in his tweets false, yet a study from Media Matters in America found that 65 percent of the time, news outlets retweet them without correcting the false claims. As *Wired* magazine noted, "If you're worried about foreign governments mounting disinformation campaigns, restricting paid political advertising on social media will do almost nothing … When foreign intelligence services want to misinform American voters, they mostly rely on Americans to do the work of spreading their messages for free."[11]

It's clear that the internet is here to stay, so many people agree that political campaigns conducted on the internet need oversight and reform. However, few agree on the best way to go about it. Some believe companies should be free to police themselves; others say that hasn't worked so far and laws should be passed to make internet political ads subject to oversight the way radio, television, and print ads are. The next several years will likely be a process of trial and error as companies try to figure out how to restrict the spread of misleading information and unfair targeting practices without harming the fairness and equality of campaign outreach.

Your Opinion Matters!

1. Do you think microtargeted ads are a big problem in politics?

2. Think about political ads you've seen or heard. Have any of them made you want to vote for someone? Have any of them made you not want to vote for someone? Explain your answers.

3. Why is dark advertising so dangerous? What, if anything, can be done about it?

PUBLIC IMAGE AND VOTER PERCEPTION

Radio and television did more to change political campaigns than simply allow candidates to reach a lot of voters at once. For many voters, it was the first time they were seeing and hearing the candidates. Suddenly, a candidate's political ideas alone weren't enough to win them voters; they also had to look and act in a way that voters saw as trustworthy, dignified, and mature. This was especially true on television.

The first nationally televised debate between two presidential candidates took place on September 26, 1960, and it forever changed the way candidates presented themselves to voters. Richard Nixon, who was the vice president at the time, was running against Senator John F. Kennedy. People had seen presidential candidates before, but this was the first time they got to watch the way they talked and reacted to things for more than a few minutes. In debates, candidates prepare as much as they can, but they can never know exactly what questions they will be called upon to answer or what their opponents are going to say. Nixon had recently come out of the hospital after a knee injury, so he looked pale and slightly ill during the debate. He also refused to wear stage makeup. In contrast, Kennedy, who had opted for the makeup, looked young and healthy. This debate is credited with helping Kennedy pull

Many people believe that the fact that the 1960 presidential debate was televised cost Nixon (*right*) the election because viewers thought Kennedy (*left*) looked healthier and more confident.

far enough ahead to win the presidency. After, candidates learned the importance of always looking and sounding good in front of the camera.

Looking Good

Presidential candidates are perhaps the most photographed, interviewed, and recorded politicians in the United States. There's a very specific image that these candidates and their parties want to express. Political parties and the candidates themselves work tirelessly throughout the campaign to maintain an image that will earn them votes at the polling stations.

Good pictures are important to a presidential candidate because they can be shared and seen instantly by millions of people, evoking immediate responses. To convey the idea that they're trustworthy and dignified, candidates use good pictures of themselves in their promotions. A bad picture can be strategically used to make the candidate look foolish and sway voters to the opposition's side. Even in interviews and debates, voters are judging how the candidate performs as much as the ideas they're sharing. In fact, one 2009 study found that people who saw candidates on film didn't remember the exact words that they said; instead, they were more affected by the way the candidate acted and carried themselves. Public image is often strictly controlled by a campaign, and candidates generally have a variety of consultants that cover not only fashion but also how a candidate speaks and acts.

While some people may not realize it, the pictures and videos that candidates appear in are often strictly designed and controlled. For example, a presidential candidate might have an interview filmed in their cozy, bright home surrounded by their spouse and children. The public image they want to convey with this is one that makes the public feel comfortable with them. They want to show that they care about family and have a secure home.

Other things candidates must consider include their clothing, the vehicles they drive, and their hairstyle. One study found that more than 30 percent of Americans choose who they're voting for based on the candidate's public image alone. Some people feel this

People who dislike Donald Trump and want to make him look silly may use a picture similar to the one on the left. In contrast, people who support him and want to show him looking more dignified and likable may use a picture similar to the one on the right.

is concerning; they would prefer that people vote for a candidate based on their policies alone. Others say that since the president represents the United States to other world leaders, a respectable public image is equally as important as strong political policies.

Creating a Public Image

Two types of public image exist in political campaigns. The first is short-term public image, which is tailored to fit a specific campaign. This is important for candidates who are running for the first time and need to quickly let voters get a sense of who they are. The other type is long-term public image, which is an image a politician has built and maintained over many years.

In a 2000 study, researchers broke down the process of building a public image into four different parts. When a candidate sets out to run a campaign, at least two of these four parts are required if a public image is going to be built successfully. The first, fundamental image, consists of all the ways a candidate acts as well as the principles and policies they stand behind. Essentially, fundamental image is the way in which voters will immediately perceive the candidate. The second, internal image, is all the private ways in which a candidate gains support within their own political party. The way they portray themselves to their party supporters is often different than the way they portray themselves to undecided voters.

External image is similar to internal image, but on a larger scale. With the candidate fully backed by their political party, they now set out to connect with the public through the media. The aim here is to promote both the political party and the presidential candidate, improving relations with voters. Unattainable image is the last level of public image building. This is all the ways in which a candidate's upbringing affects their behavior. This upbringing includes their educational background, their cultural background, and any factors that motivate their work.

A candidate's style is an important part of their public image. This is something that goes beyond their hairstyle or clothing. Style is how the candidate carries and presents themselves to the American people. A candidate may have one kind of style with one group of voters and another kind of style with a different group, depending on what kind of image they think each group wants to see. However, speeches and televised debates are two events that show the same style to many voters at once. One candidate may have an agreeable and accepting quality about them, making their style seem kind and easygoing. Some voters may want that kind of president. In contrast, an opposing candidate could come across as aggressive and abrupt. Voters who interpret this style as tough and no-nonsense may prefer this kind of president instead.

Many different things contribute to creating a candidate's style and public image. The *International Journal of Scientific & Engineering Research* explained in 2014 that "the style of the electoral campaign is a collection of the speeches of the candidates for performing public matters, the press conferences, the performances of the candidate or his representatives in the media, the commercials

American Cultural Influences

There's no such thing as the "ideal" president for all voters. Different voters want different things. However, there are some things most voters like more than others. For example, many voters respond to candidates who seem "normal" and down-to-earth. They tend to dislike candidates who seem elitist, meaning they portray an image that, intentionally or not, makes voters feel the candidate thinks they're better than the average citizen. Candidates have to walk a very fine line in the type of persona they create, appearing intelligent enough to do the job but not so intelligent that they're seen as elitist. The amount of wealth a candidate has can also play into this; most voters don't like candidates who seem out of touch with the lives of regular citizens because they worry that it means the candidate isn't listening to voters' concerns.

In her book *The Partly Cloudy Patriot*, Sarah Vowell used the 2000 presidential race between Al Gore and George W. Bush as an example of how important image is. An article in the *Los Angeles Times* described their first debate: "Gore studied hard and was thoroughly prepared for the televised civics and government quizzes each debate provided. A teacher might have given him an A. But much of the rest of the class just wanted to punch Mr. Smarty-Pants in the nose."[1] Vowell questioned why people had such a strong dislike of a presidential candidate who was clearly intelligent and prepared for his debate. She mentioned that, since being president is a difficult job, it would make sense to elect someone very intelligent. By informally studying the way Gore portrayed himself and the way other people wrote about him at the time, she came to the conclusion that the way Gore portrayed his knowledge made voters feel as if he thought he were smarter and better than them. Although he had the knowledge and experience necessary to potentially be a good president, his style ultimately may have cost him the election. Vowell wrote, "American democracy is tough. When one of a culture's guiding credos [beliefs] is that 'all men are created equal,' any person ... who distinguishes himself through mental excellence, is a nuisance."[2]

1. Quoted in Sarah Vowell, *The Partly Cloudy Patriot* (New York, NY: Simon & Schuster, 2002), p. 101.

2. Vowell, *The Partly Cloudy Patriot*, p. 112–13.

being used, the presence at public events during the campaign, saluting supporters etc."[1] In each new election, voters are looking for someone very specific to lead their country.

The Role of the Media

Video—on television, YouTube, other social media platforms, or a streaming service—remains one of the primary ways of reaching large numbers of voters at once. News networks have one goal: to gain viewers so the network can attract advertisers who will pay the network money to air their ads. Networks must constantly compete in order to gain the upper hand. What this means during elections, however, is that the media often posts stories that draw negative attention. Negative attention that stirs debate is far more likely to draw viewers than positive attention. Of course, this can be helpful for some candidates and harmful for others. Candidates getting widespread media attention become more recognizable, and recognition makes people more likely to vote for that candidate. What one voter sees as negative may be seen as positive by another, and while candidates generally prefer positive coverage to negative, they also may prefer negative coverage to no coverage.

The media depicts candidates in various ways depending on how they want to influence viewers. All news outlets have at least a little bit of bias. Some hide it fairly well, while others don't even try. The words a reporter uses, the photos they choose of a candidate, and the facts they choose to highlight can all be used to sway voters' opinions in one direction or another. For example, a 2018 study from Oxford University found that during the campaign process for the 2016 election, "Clinton was portrayed with more expressions of happiness, which rendered her as more favorable, whereas Trump was associated with more expressions of anger, which made him look less positive but more dominant."[2]

News outlets rarely tell people exactly what to think, but they can subtly change how a voter views a candidate. A 2017 study by the Pew Research Center looked at the ways negative and positive statements about a president can affect people's opinions about them. The researchers showed participants two different kinds of news stories: Some had twice as many positive statements about Trump as negative statements, while the others had twice as many negative statements as positive ones. Viewers assessed Trump more positively after the positive news reports, while the opposite was true for those who saw the negative news reports of him.

The aim of this study was not to determine if news networks were being biased; instead, it was looking more at the viewing habits of voting Americans. Voters who want to see more positive coverage of their president will watch news networks that provide those kinds of stories. Those who prefer more criticisms of the current administration will choose to view news outlets that do exactly that. People tend to choose sources that align with their own biases, whether those are conservative or liberal. This means people often don't see the other side of the story.

Another problem with the media is that, regardless of bias, sometimes the whole story simply doesn't get reported. In *The Partly Cloudy Patriot*, Sarah Vowell described a visit Al Gore made on the campaign trail to a media literacy class at Concord High School in Concord, New Hampshire. Although Gore had a reputation in the media for being stiff and unlikeable, the students didn't find that to be the case. One student remembered that he had

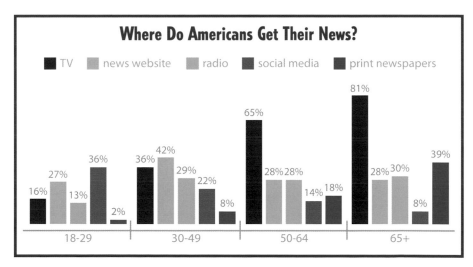

As this information from the Pew Research Center shows, a person's age plays a big role in determining where they get their news from.

mentioned liking *The Simpsons*. Another said, "He understood that we are people ... We are kids but we're not dumb. We understand what's going on, and he respected that."[3] He spoke on the topic of violence in schools in a way that many of the students found inspiring, encouraging them to get involved and telling them that their actions could make a difference.

Later, the news didn't report any of these moments. Instead, a reporter misheard Gore at one point and thought he was taking credit for something he had never done. This story was the one that was printed and got national attention. Gore was mocked on late-night entertainment shows and criticized by multiple reporters. The students were shocked at how mishearing one word had made such a difference between the way the story was reported and the way they had experienced it themselves. Vowell suspected that, since Gore already had a reputation for claiming credit for things he didn't do—he'd famously been mocked for claiming to have invented the internet—the reporters heard what they wanted to hear and published the story that fit with the image Gore already had. When Vowell asked 16-year-old student Ashley Pettengill "what we lose when the press omits descriptions of how a candidate might actually make a good president, she answers, 'I think we miss out on every reason to vote for them.'"[4]

Voters often need to rely on reporters to give them information that helps them decide who to vote for. It's impossible for each individual voter to be at every public appearance and private campaign party to see for themselves how a candidate acts. However, the danger with this is that, as Vowell noted, "so much political speech is lies, spin, and misrepresentation ... representatives of the news media carry around story lines of the candidates in their heads, and reporters light up when reality randomly corroborates [supports] these pictures."[5] Most of the news outlets that had misreported Gore's words later issued corrections and apologies. They weren't lying on purpose, but it's important for people to remember that reporters are human and make mistakes sometimes. It's up to voters to make informed decisions by reading articles from multiple news outlets and questioning what they're told.

Presidents and the Press

Although campaigns can largely control how the candidate presents themselves, they can't control the media, which can post or report on anything they wish about the candidate. News outlets need to tell the truth, although they can spin it in certain ways. However, entertainment shows can say anything as long as it's clearly a joke. Presidents throughout history have struggled with this dynamic, which can both damage and help their political careers. Thomas Jefferson, for instance, served as president during a time when American newspapers attacked politicians and openly took sides. Although he wrote letters denouncing the credibility of newspapers, he sometimes used their bias to his advantage during a messy campaign against John Adams.

In the early 1970s, President Richard Nixon went further than Jefferson. He not only denounced the press, he also actively tried to shut down a television station that was owned by the *Washington Post*. This newspaper had broken the news of what came to be known as the Watergate scandal. On June 17, 1972, burglars were caught and arrested in the Watergate complex, where the Democratic National Committee was headquartered. The burglars were soon linked to Nixon's reelection campaign. Nixon tried covering up the events at Watergate, fearing that he would be impeached, but the press reported it anyway. Because shutting down a TV station was a clear violation of free speech rights, Nixon didn't succeed in his censorship attempts.

One of the most vocal presidential opponents of certain media outlets in recent years has been Donald Trump. Trump has openly called for action against the media numerous times, frequently deeming them "fake news." In many cases, though, the stories Trump was denouncing were true. It's important for people to understand what fake news truly is. The news changes every day, and what's initially reported as true may turn out to be wrong or incomplete later as more facts emerge. This doesn't make the original story fake news; reporters release stories as facts come in, and responsible journalists will note in their articles when more information is needed. As in the case of the Al Gore story,

Nixon was unable to stop the press from reporting the Watergate scandal. Knowing the evidence was against him, he chose to resign instead of facing impeachment.

reporters also sometimes make mistakes, and again, a responsible news outlet will issue corrections when it finds out it printed something wrong. Instead, something that is truly fake news is knowingly made up and never corrected later. It's a deliberate lie intended to fool people, and it's not meant to be taken as a joke. Some people believe Trump and other politicians use the term fake news to discredit news stories they don't like or don't agree with instead of actually calling out real instances of fake news. This is why it's important for people to have a strong understanding of what fake news is and is not.

Your Opinion Matters!

1. Think about recent presidential candidates. How did their public image influence the way you thought about them?

2. What qualities are important to you in a president? What kind of image would make you most likely to vote for someone?

3. How can you do your best to make sure you're getting all the facts about a presidential candidate rather than fake news and biased reporting?

THE FIGHT AGAINST CORRUPTION

Experts agree that corruption is a problem that continues to plague American elections, even though laws have been passed to attempt to control it. Campaign finance reform is something that's frequently discussed in the media, and many candidates make it part of their platform. However, because politicians are the ones passing the laws and they tend to benefit from the corruption in the system, it's been difficult to get reform laws passed.

Another problem with the American voting system is a long history of voter suppression that continues to this day. Some politicians pass laws that they claim are designed to prevent voter fraud. In most instances, however, the unspoken aim of the law is to stop certain people—generally people who would vote against the candidate—from casting their vote.

Campaign Finance Laws

As the costs of running a campaign for elected office have steadily increased to levels that make campaigning unaffordable for all but the richest people, candidates are pressured to raise huge amounts of money if they want to have any hope of successfully running for office or being reelected. Numerous reforms have been passed, but some campaigns have found new ways to get around each new legal

◀ People are still fighting against voter suppression today.

requirement, allowing large amounts of private money to continue to pour into congressional and presidential elections. In fact, commentators sometimes describe campaign finance as "legal corruption" because contributions are technically legal under existing campaign finance laws.

There are many laws in place as of 2020 that govern campaign finance. The FEC oversees and enforces these laws, which include publicly disclosing how campaign funds are spent, disclosing how tax money is being used to pay for presidential candidates' expenses, and restricting the amount of money raised and spent for a campaign. This type of oversight is necessary for several reasons. Limits on the amount a candidate can spend on their own campaign are meant to make it easier for people who aren't millionaires to win. However, since the cap is set at $50,000, less wealthy candidates must rely more on donations from supporters. This comes with its own rules and problems.

Many donations or a single large donation from one source can be used by the donor to encourage the candidate to vote in a way that favors the donor and their chosen causes. For this reason, there are many limits on how much one person or group can give in a calendar year to a candidate. For example, political action committees (PACs) are only allowed to give $5,000 to a specific campaign committee per election. However, there are also many loopholes in these spending laws. For instance, a PAC can also give $15,000 per year to a political party, which can then spend that money on its chosen candidate. There are also super PACs, which have only been in existence since a 2010 federal court decision. Super PACs can raise as much money as they want from any source—including companies, unions, and individuals—and spend as much money as they want on a candidate's campaign. However, they are slightly limited in that they can't donate the money directly to the candidate, and they can't talk to the candidates about what they're doing with that money. For instance, a super PAC could raise $10,000 and use it to pay for ads that support Candidate A and oppose Candidate B, but they're not allowed to ask Candidate A what they should say in the ads.

The problem many people have with current campaign finance laws is that there are many loopholes that allow wealthy individuals and special interest groups to quietly give large amounts of money to their chosen candidate. For example, using a technique called bundling, individuals or companies can collect contributions from family members, friends, or employees and then deliver the combined donation to a particular candidate with a clear understanding that it is all coming from one place. This makes candidates as beholden to that person or company as if they had directly made the large donation, all while still abiding by the law that no more than a certain amount can come from any individual.

In the last few years, for instance, many people have been looking closely at the amount of money politicians take from the National Rifle Association (NRA). The number of

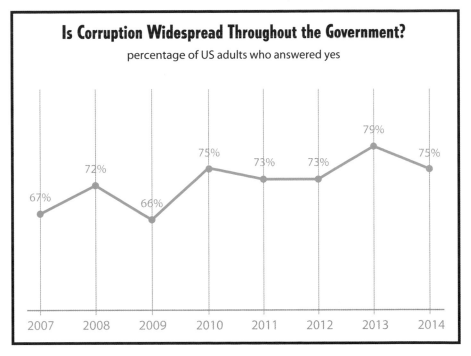

Is Corruption Widespread Throughout the Government?

percentage of US adults who answered yes

67% 72% 66% 75% 73% 73% 79% 75%

2007 2008 2009 2010 2011 2012 2013 2014

About three-quarters of the US population believe government corruption is a widespread problem, as this information from Gallup shows. Campaign finance reform is one way people are fighting to reduce corruption in the government.

shootings in public places, especially schools, has been increasing in the United States, and many have called for stricter gun control laws. Some politicians agree, but others have stated that restrictions wouldn't have any effect on the number of shootings. In many cases, these politicians who stand against stronger gun control laws have received large campaign donations from the NRA over a number of years. For example, Florida senator Marco Rubio has received more than $3 million from the NRA over the course of his career, according to the *LA Times*. In the wake of the February 2018 Marjory Stoneman Douglas High School shooting in Parkland, Florida, Rubio made statements that indicated he was unsure whether stricter laws would have prevented the tragedy from happening, despite data from other countries around the world showing that the amount of shootings decreased after laws were passed that made it harder to get guns. The NRA's donations have affected other policy decisions as well. For instance, in 2015, 54 senators voted against a bill that would forbid people on the government's terrorist watch list from purchasing a gun. These senators had collectively received $37 million from the NRA.

On an episode of the popular HBO show *Last Week Tonight with John Oliver*, Senator Chris Murphy raised an important point about where legislators' money comes from. He said he targets people who can easily afford to give $1,000, which means the issues these donors want their representatives to address are very different than the issues people who live in poverty want to see addressed.

All this money buys enormous access to Congress as well as to other government officials—close contact that ordinary citizens don't have. This access may buy officials' votes or sway decisions on key policies and pieces of legislation, but often, the more common outcome is much more subtle: influence. In Congress, this might take several different forms. A politician might vote to prevent bills or certain parts of bills from ever being reported outside of congressional committees, or they might quietly add a rider that benefits a private interest into larger bills that are sure to pass. A rider is a provision that has little or no connection to a bill; it's a way to get laws that have little support passed. For instance, a bill about education reform might include a rider that gives tax cuts to a corporation. Financial influence might also convince government officials to block or change government regulations, influence regulatory decisions, help secure government contract awards, or achieve some other form of behind-the-scenes advocacy that benefits campaign donors.

Close examination of corruption in American politics makes one thing plain: The general public suffers most from it. Reformers

Corruption and Image

There are many different factors that determine how corruption affects a candidate's public image. Was the politician directly linked to a crime, or were they merely implicated? Did the politician serve jail time, or were they acquitted?

Interestingly, charges of corruption don't always mean that a politician's political career is over. In some cases, they are able to recover their public image—maybe not fully, but enough to enjoy the rest of their career. For others, corruption scandals cause their popularity to dip so low that they choose to resign from their position. In very rare cases, the corruption is considered severe enough to warrant impeachment, which is a charge of misconduct or criminal behavior brought against a government official, such as the president. After the official is impeached, a trial is held to determine whether the accusations are true and serious enough to justify removal from office.

In United States history, only three presidents have been impeached: Andrew Johnson in 1868, Bill Clinton in 1998, and Donald Trump in 2019. Richard Nixon resigned rather than face impeachment. So far, no president has been removed from office following impeachment. The crimes Trump and Nixon faced impeachment for had to do with inappropriately using their presidential power to influence their reelection campaigns. While Nixon's scandal and near-impeachment ended his political career, many of Trump's supporters have remained loyal to him despite the incriminating evidence that has been brought against him.

say big money in politics unquestionably results in government policies that are geared toward the needs of corporate contributors rather than the needs of ordinary citizens. These effects are often very difficult to prove, and most of the time they're hidden from the general public. Sometimes, however, information about this system leaks out, resulting in much-publicized scandals and causing the public to suspect all politicians of corruption.

Barriers to Reform

Although many people have called for campaign finance reform, it has been slow in coming, and there have been many setbacks and barriers. After the Watergate scandal, the Federal Elections Campaign Act (FECA) put new laws into place, but they were challenged in a 1976 Supreme Court case called *Buckley v. Valeo*. Specifically, the ruling eliminated all of FECA's spending limits, as well as limits on contributions made by candidates themselves or made by citizens or PACs for so-called independent expenditures, such as advertising that was not connected with a candidate's campaign. The Court's reasoning was that these limits were an unconstitutional limit on free speech—a claim many experts have challenged. The Court upheld the remaining parts of FECA, which included its disclosure requirements, the public financing program, and the individual, party, and PAC limits on direct campaign contributions.

Experts claim that the court decision unleashed a new wave of corporate money onto elections; the decision allowed unlimited amounts to be spent on campaigns and created a climate in which wealthy candidates were more successful in running for office. Also, by introducing the concept of independent expenditures, *Buckley v. Valeo* encouraged a whole new trend of expensive television advertisements, called issue ads, paid for by PACs set up by corporations and other special interest groups. As long as the ads were independent—meaning they didn't coordinate directly with campaigns or use any of a list of words that the Supreme Court said would constitute express advocacy on behalf of or against a candidate (such as "vote for," "elect," or "defeat")—there was absolutely no limit to the amount of money that could be spent. In recent years, people have stretched the legal definition of an issue ad by simply avoiding the specific words mentioned by the Supreme Court, blurring the line between issue advocacy and express advocacy. For example, many people are familiar with ads that run during an election year that say things such as, "Candidate A supports policies that are bad for small businesses. Candidate B opposes those policies." As long as the ad doesn't specifically tell people to elect Candidate B, it's technically considered an issue ad even though it's clearly supporting a particular candidate. The disclaimer the FEC requires on advocacy ads isn't required on issue ads, which means it's harder for people who hear or see the ad to know who's trying to influence their opinion. This is a loophole in the law that many candidates have taken advantage of since it was passed, allowing them to spend millions of dollars on campaign advertising, getting around the law that was intended to limit that spending.

The Voter Fraud Myth

Campaign fundraising isn't the only part of the election process that has fallen prey to corruption. Voter suppression is also widespread, and it mainly affects people of color.

Voter suppression—tricks designed to stop people from exercising their legal right to vote—is nothing new. Black men gained the right to vote in 1870, but various "Jim Crow" laws were passed that were explicitly designed to prevent them from doing so. One such law created a poll tax, which was money a person had to pay in order to vote and which was generally set higher than most black people could afford. Another was a literacy test. Since most former slaves had never been taught how to read or write, many failed the literacy test, and those who passed it might be told they had failed anyway. A third was the "grandfather clause," which said people could only avoid the poll tax, literacy test, or other requirements if their grandfather had been allowed to vote. This rule was specifically passed to reduce the voting burden on white people who were poor or illiterate while keeping it in place for black people.

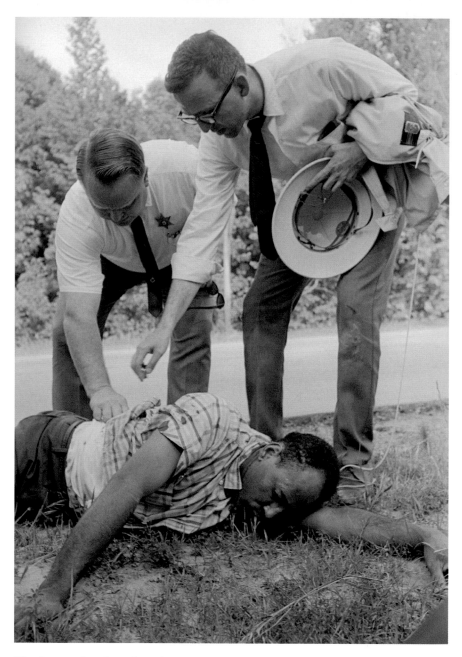

Black people often faced violence when they tried to exercise their rights. Shown here is student and civil rights activist James Meredith, who was shot and wounded in 1966 for encouraging black people to register to vote.

In 1965, the Voting Rights Act outlawed such voter suppression laws. One of the main parts of this law said that states had to get federal approval before they changed their election laws. This part of the Voting Rights Act was struck down by the Supreme Court in 2013; the Court claimed it was no longer necessary because racism in the United States had decreased to the point where no states would try to pass voter suppression laws. However, this proved to be false.

Voter suppression today looks slightly different than it did in the past. People of color and poor people are still disproportionately targeted, but the people who pass these laws claim this isn't the intention. Instead, politicians work to convince the public that the laws protect against voter fraud, which they say is widespread and a serious problem. Voter fraud covers several crimes, including voting more than once in a single election; pretending to be someone else—for example, by registering in the name of a dead person—in order to vote; voting without being legally registered; voting in someone else's name; changing the vote count; paying people to cast a vote for a certain candidate; or pretending to help someone vote in order to force them to change their vote (for example, reading the ballot incorrectly to a blind person to trick them into voting for a candidate they don't want).

Hearing about isolated incidents of voter fraud can reinforce in people's minds that the problem is indeed widespread and severe. Donald Trump has claimed repeatedly that fraudulent votes caused him to lose the popular vote in 2016. In 2018, he claimed in an interview that Democrats were only winning elections because of voter fraud, saying that voters sometimes "go to their car, put on a different hat, put on a different shirt, come in and vote again."[1] However, numerous studies have found that this is not the case. In January 2017, the nonpartisan Brennan Center for Justice wrote, "putting rhetoric aside to look at the facts makes clear that fraud by voters at the polls is vanishingly rare, and does not happen on a scale even close to that necessary to 'rig' an election."[2] A 2014 study by the

Concerns about voter fraud are high in the United States, but studies show that it almost never happens.

Washington Post found just over 30 possible instances of voter impersonation fraud out of a billion ballots. A similar study in 2012 looked at every state's voting records in a 12-year period, finding only 10 cases of voter impersonation fraud within that time. Numerous government agencies, including the Supreme Court, have come to the same conclusion: Instances of voter fraud are incredibly rare.

Voter Suppression Laws Today

Despite these facts, many states have passed laws that they say are aimed at preventing voter fraud but actually work to stop voters from exercising their legal rights. Voter identification (ID) laws are one example. To many people, it makes sense that someone should show their driver's license or other government-issued

ID when they vote. However, because it's so incredibly rare for someone to pretend to be another person in order to vote, these laws don't solve any problems; they only hurt legitimate voters. The American Civil Liberties Union (ACLU) explained the problems with voter ID laws:

- *Millions of Americans Lack ID. 11 [percent] of U.S. citizens—or more than 21 million Americans—do not have government-issued photo identification.*

- *Obtaining ID Costs Money. Even if ID is offered for free, voters must incur numerous costs (such as paying for birth certificates) to apply for a government-issued ID …*
    - o *The travel required is often a major burden on people with disabilities, the elderly, or those in rural areas without access to a car or public transportation …*

- *Minority voters disproportionately lack ID. Nationally, up to 25 [percent] of African-American citizens of voting age lack government-issue photo ID, compared to only 8 [percent] of whites.*

- *States exclude forms of ID in a discriminatory manner … Until its voter ID law was struck down, North Carolina prohibited public assistance IDs and state employee ID cards, which are disproportionately held by Black voters …*

- *So-called cases of in-person impersonation voter "fraud" are almost always the product of an elections worker or voter making an honest mistake, and … even these mistakes are extremely infrequent.*[3]

Overall, the ACLU reported that voter ID laws reduce voter turnout, especially among people of color. Another voter ID law was passed by North Dakota in 2018. This one states that a voter must have a residential street address on their ID in order for it to be accepted. At first, this might seem sensible; people may think, *Of course someone should have to prove they actually live where they're trying to vote.* However, many people are unaware that this law disenfranchises, or takes away the right to vote from, many

Gerrymandering

Gerrymandering, or "the practice of drawing the boundaries of electoral districts in a way that gives one political party an unfair advantage over its rivals ... or that dilutes the voting power of members of ethnic or linguistic minority groups,"[1] is a form of voter suppression that has been used for decades. In 1812, Massachusetts governor Elbridge Gerry signed a bill that changed the shape of several senatorial districts in Massachusetts. This was done in an attempt to get members of the Democratic-Republican Party elected over members of the Federalist Party. Some people thought one of the newly drawn districts looked like a salamander, and after a political cartoon mockingly called it a "gerrymander," the name stuck.

Today, US courts continue to hear arguments for and against cases of gerrymandering. As of 2020, political gerrymandering is often decided on a case-by-case basis; sometimes the courts rule that it is legal, while other times they rule that it is illegal.

1. Brian Duignan, "Gerrymandering," *Encyclopaedia Britannica*, modified August 1, 2019, www.britannica.com/topic/gerrymandering.

Native Americans. Many Native American residents of North Dakota live on reservations, and those reservations are so far out in the country that the post office won't deliver mail to them. Instead, their mail is put into a post office box (P.O. box), and they must go to the post office to pick it up. A person's mailing address, not their residential address, is on their ID. Because of this law, as many as 5,000 Native Americans may lose their right to vote.

Another voter suppression law that has recently been passed in several states is called the "exact match" system. This means the name in the voter registry must exactly match the name in the state system. Again, this seems logical to many people; doesn't it make sense that someone named Tom Smith shouldn't be able to vote under the name Tom Jones? In an interview with

National Public Radio (NPR), journalist Ari Berman explained why the law is harming people—especially people of color—instead of protecting elections:

> *This kind of exact-match system is known as "disenfranchisement by typo" because when you submit a voter registration form, if you have a hyphen missing on your name, if you have an apostrophe missing, if you use "Tom" on one form and "Thomas" on another, your form is going to be blocked ... [Voting rights lawyers] told me ... that basically the names of people who are African-American or Latino or Asian-American tend to be more unfamiliar to election workers. So they might have names that don't match on the databases from one form to another, or election officials might actually enter the correct name incorrectly because they're confused by the spelling or they don't recognize the name.*[4]

Berman noted that in 2009, Georgia attempted to pass this exact match law and was denied permission by the federal government. In 2010, Brian Kemp was elected governor and began using the exact match system illegally. After the Supreme Court no longer required federal oversight for states' election law changes, Georgia reauthorized the system, making it legal. Multiple studies and court rulings have found that voter suppression laws helped Republicans win not only the presidency but also a majority of seats in Congress in 2016. Experts say this suggests Republicans who want to hang on to their power will be unwilling to change such laws.

Other laws on the books disenfranchise people who have committed a felony, or serious crime. In some states, people who have committed a felony lose their right to vote for the rest of their lives, which many people believe is unfair. They say someone who has served their time in prison has paid their debt to society and should be allowed to receive all their former rights. Another law states that people who live in certain US territories, such as Puerto Rico and Guam, are American citizens but aren't allowed to vote unless they move to one of the 50 states. Some people use outright illegal voter suppression tactics, such as

Many people believe that once someone has served their time in prison, they should get their voting rights back. Shown here at a rally for felon voting rights are three men who each served between 35 and 41 years in prison.

giving false information to certain voters to prevent them from going to the polls. For example, in 2010, Republican Robert Ehrlich was running for governor of Maryland against the incumbent governor, Democrat Martin O'Malley. Consultants for Ehrlich's campaign called 110,000 registered black Democrat voters on the afternoon of Election Day to falsely tell them O'Malley had already won, so they didn't have to bother voting. This was ruled a clear example of racially motivated voter suppression. Additionally, as false rumors spread that undocumented immigrants are voting in large numbers, 1 in 10 Latinx citizens report being illegally harassed and intimidated when they show up to vote, as some other voters assume they're undocumented.

The fight for equal voting rights for all American citizens—and for the ability to freely exercise those rights—will likely continue for many years.

Your Opinion Matters!

1. What campaign finance reform laws would you pass if you were in charge, and why?

2. Do you feel that voter fraud is a serious issue in US elections? Explain your answer.

3. Give some examples that aren't in the book of how voter ID laws could prevent someone from voting.

CHAPTER FIVE

THE FUTURE OF CAMPAIGNING IN AMERICA

The road to Election Day in the near future may look very different than it does today. New ways of voting and becoming involved on Election Day are already being tested, but on a small scale. Generational differences and political divides are also changing the way people vote and, therefore, the way candidates choose to campaign toward voters. Political parties are becoming more unified, which means that they're voting together on policies and social issues that at one time divided their party. New technology is being unveiled all the time, and candidates are finding creative—and occasionally unethical or illegal—ways to put it to use. While it's impossible to predict exactly what will happen in the future, we can look at what's happening right now to get a general idea.

Changes in Voter Demographics

With each new election comes a new political landscape that shapes who people will vote into office. The voting patterns the nation is seeing today may look very different in future elections. For example, more young people are voting today. In 2019, the Pew Research Center reported that more people between the ages of 18 and 53 voted in 2018 than people older than 53. This is a relatively new trend;

◀ Kids can get involved in the political process before they're even old enough to vote.

according to the *Washington Post*, 36 percent of voters ages 18 to 29 voted in the 2018 midterm elections, compared to 20 percent in the 2014 midterms. Typically, young people are less likely to vote than older people. There are a number of reasons for this. Historically, many young people tend to be less interested in politics; others feel their vote doesn't count, so they don't bother. However, organizations such as Rock the Vote and HeadCount have run campaigns to encourage young people to register and vote, and social media users often share posts urging people to show up to the polls to make their voices heard. Additionally, issues such as gun control have spurred young adults to start taking a more active interest in politics and to commit to voting for politicians who share their values.

The reason all of this changes campaigns is because politicians cater to their largest voting base. Lately, in the United States, that has been the oldest segment of society simply because they're far more likely to show up to the polls. However, if more young people show up and vote, politicians will need to start paying more attention to those voters' concerns if they want to win. Their numbers will only grow in the future as more people turn 18. According to the Pew Research Center, in 2020, Generation Z will account for fully 10 percent of eligible voters—not an insignificant number, especially when added to the number of millennial voters.

The same is true for people of color, whose demographic is also growing, thanks partially to immigration. Although some local elections allow immigrants and noncitizens to vote, this is rare. However, every day, immigrants are completing the naturalization process to become American citizens and earn the right to vote in all elections. As with young people, addressing the concerns of voters of color can make or break a candidate's campaign. For example, in 2013, the Center for American Progress estimated that 73 percent of Asian American voters and 71 percent of Latinx voters supported President Obama for his 2012 reelection. Immigration reform policies, which were a major point of focus on the campaign trail,

Many politicians have started to realize that they must appeal to young people as well as people of color if they want to win an election.

resonated with these groups. In the past, people of color were called minority groups, but the Center for American Progress noted that demographics have changed in the United States to the point where there is no clear majority among the various races.

An App for Soldiers

In the 2016 presidential election, only about 20 percent of military service members voted. There are many soldiers who want to vote, but it's difficult to do from overseas. Absentee ballots, which are submitted via mail for people in these situations, are very hard to receive and send out in the middle of a war zone. In 2016, CNN reported that West Virginia was unveiling a new app to help make it easier for overseas citizens to vote.

The company behind the development of the app, Voatz, is one of several companies looking to change the future of voting. The app itself had a variety of security features, such as requiring service members to upload a photo of their government-issued ID as well as take a video of themselves. Other safeguards were in place to reduce the chance of hacking. Despite these safeguards, many election experts as well as computer security experts have denounced the idea of voting by app, so it's unlikely to become widespread any time soon.

Fears About Election Integrity

New technology is changing the ways people cast their votes. For example, digital voting machines are now very common, and computers help tally the votes. However, many experts have voiced concerns about this system. Some have argued that America's networks and servers can have problems that mean votes might not be accurately recorded and counted. Others fear that voting over the internet will open the door to hacking, malware, and other interference.

Most places use at least one kind of computer technology in the voting process. In some places, people fill out a paper ballot and scan it into a machine. In others, people go into a booth and make their selections directly on a computer. Many people think it's only natural that voting options keep up with the technological times; paper ballots are often seen as outdated, and most election officials swear all the voting machines are secure and accurate. However, there are serious problems with digital voting.

In 2019, a segment on *Last Week Tonight with John Oliver* looked at some of the problems with electronic forms of voting. One issue was with the voting machines themselves. Some have been known to miscount votes, produce extra votes, or otherwise malfunction. In the 2016 election, many had not been tested before they were shipped from the manufacturing center to the polling places. Election Day volunteers are not chosen for their knowledge of computers, so it's unlikely they would know how to fix a machine if it broke down while people were voting.

Other problems relate to security. One reporter hacked a voting machine in under two minutes—without using any special tools—to illustrate how insecure that type of machine is. Many states don't bother updating the software on their machines regularly, and many voting machines are connected to the internet. Both of these situations leave the machines vulnerable to hackers. Furthermore, it's often difficult or impossible for officials to tell when hacking has occurred, meaning someone could tamper with millions of votes without leaving any evidence behind.

Because of all these issues, experts say paper ballots are the best and most secure voting method, even though they may seem outdated. An act introduced to Congress in 2019 would require the whole country to return to paper ballots, but opposition to the act in the Republican-controlled Senate makes it unlikely to be passed any time soon. However, presidential candidates are listening to people's concerns, and most of the candidates for the 2020 election supported requiring paper ballots. Only Democratic candidate Andrew Yang did not; he said that his preferred voting method is via a secure app. While such an app would increase voter turnout and accessibility, the same security concerns remain.

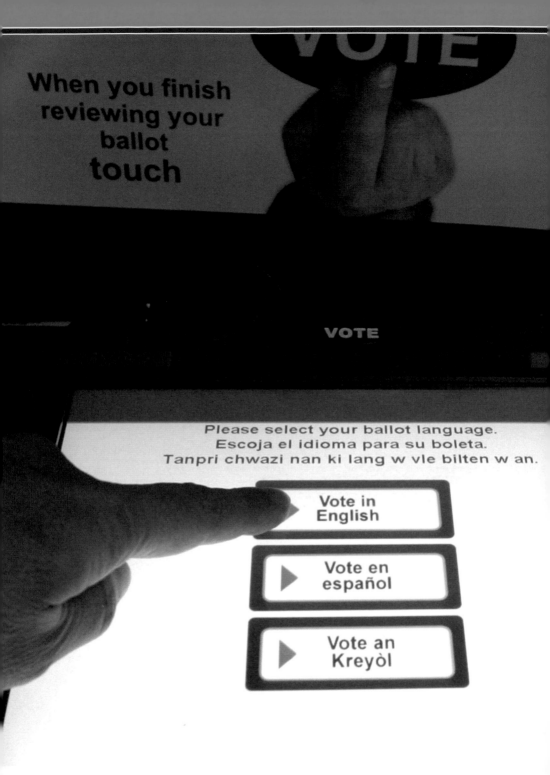

Some polling places use touchscreen voting machines. Others use a machine that counts votes by scanning paper ballots. Technology experts have expressed concerns about the security of both types of machines.

Using New Technology to Campaign

Technology is changing not only the way people cast their votes but also the ways politicians campaign. Historically, as soon as a new technology has become available, candidates have incorporated it into their campaigns. In 2008, for instance, Obama's campaign initiated the first widespread use of websites, email, and social networking in a presidential campaign. All of these became important tools to get voters involved in fundraising, organizing events locally, and increasing voter registration. Candidates have always gathered data on voters and used that to target their campaigns, but the current technological era makes this easier than ever to do.

Some political campaigns have created new programs to analyze the social media activity of users who interacted at some point with their campaign. Social media behavior can give political campaigns a wealth of personal user information. This information is then used to show users specific ads and pages that relate to the campaign, the candidate, and the candidate's agenda. For example, according to PolitiFact, "The Obama campaign created a Facebook app for supporters to donate, learn of voting requirements, and find nearby houses to canvass. The app asked users' permission to scan their photos, friends lists, and news feeds. Most users complied."[1] These users knew the app was collecting their information, but this isn't always the case with internet apps. The lack of laws for regulating the tracking and sale of such information has recently been a major point of discussion in the media.

Facebook and the Cambridge Analytica Scandal

Starting around 2014, a company named Cambridge Analytica worked with Donald Trump and his team on his presidential campaign. The company's business model is gathering data on people and selling it to other people or companies—in this case, the Trump campaign—to create ads targeted toward specific groups of people. For example, someone who posts about supporting Trump might start seeing ads encouraging them to send money to the campaign. This in and of itself was not illegal, but the way Cambridge Analytica went about gathering information may have been.

In 2014, a researcher named Aleksandr Kogan created a third-party personality quiz app for Facebook called This Is Your Digital Life. When people downloaded and used this app and took the quiz, they gave Kogan access to their personal data and their friends'. This was legal under Facebook's terms

Former Cambridge Analytica employee Christopher Wylie was the one who exposed the company's actions. This photo of Wylie was taken in 2018, when he testified before the Senate committee on this issue.

of service because the app permissions clearly stated what was going to be collected. People who clicked "agree" to the permissions—whether they read them first or not—legally gave Kogan the ability to gather their data as well as their friends' data, even though their friends had no idea this was happening and weren't given the chance to agree or disagree to it. Kogan later sold the information to Cambridge Analytica, which violated Facebook's terms of service and may have been illegal. The company got in trouble because it kept and used this information without the permission of the people it had been gathered from.

When employee Christopher Wylie realized what was happening, he quit because he felt the company's actions were immoral. He stated that he tried to warn officials about what the company was doing, but no one paid attention until after Trump won the election. Cambridge Analytica executives were later caught on video bragging that their actions had helped Trump get elected. Kogan has stated that this wasn't possible with the data he had collected, but it's unclear whether or not this is true. Facebook had already faced controversy regarding the 2016 presidential election; it was accused of not doing enough to identify and remove fake news articles shared by Russian trolls. The Cambridge Analytica scandal refueled fears that Facebook wasn't doing enough to protect its users' privacy, and CEO Mark Zuckerberg was called to testify before Congress. Facebook wasn't shut down, but it did lose thousands of users who were worried about their privacy.

Due to all the negative attention surrounding it, Cambridge Analytica ceased operations in May 2018, only five years after it had been founded. However, experts say this scenario is likely to happen again now that candidates know it's possible. Digital data collection and microtargeting are fueling the future of political campaigns.

The Journey to Election Day Continues

The long road to Election Day has seen countless changes over the past 230 years. New technology, new legislation, and new candidates are constantly changing the campaign process. While many of the changes have made voting more accessible and fair to the general public, there is still so much more that needs to be changed. Election Day, however, is deeply entrenched in tradition and complicated processes. Changes won't happen overnight, but voters can advocate for campaign and election reforms that they feel are best for themselves and the country.

Your Opinion Matters!

1. What voting methods do you think we should use? Explain your answer.

2. Are you concerned about your data being used by campaigns? Why or why not?

3. What are some other ways you think future political campaigns might change?

GETTING INVOLVED

The following are some suggestions for taking what you've just read and applying that information to your everyday life.

- Volunteer with a voter registration campaign.

- Encourage your eligible friends and relatives to exercise their right to vote.

- Speak up when you hear people say things about voting or political campaigns that aren't true.

- Advocate for campaign finance reform rules that you feel strongly about.

- Learn more about voter suppression.

- Think critically about campaign ads, posts on social media, and news articles so you can spot fake or misleading information.

- Don't share things on social media about political campaigns that you haven't already researched yourself.

- Think about why you like or dislike a candidate; is it because of their policies or their image?

NOTES

Introduction: The Long Road to Election Day

1. Michael Scherer, Pratheek Rebala, and Chris Wilson, "The Incredible Rise in Campaign Spending," *TIME*, modified October 23, 2014, time.com/3534117/the-incredible-rise-in-campaign-spending.

2. Dan Patterson, "How to Hack the Midterm Election With Social Media," CBS News, September 12, 2018, www.cbsnews.com/news/how-to-hack-the-midterm-election-with-social-media.

Chapter One: Presidential Elections from Start to Finish

1. Sarah Mervosh and Matt Flegenheimer, "How Early Do Presidential Campaigns Start? Earlier Than You May Think," *New York Times*, December 31, 2018, www.nytimes.com/2018/12/31/us/politics/presidential-campaigns-2020.html.

2. Joanathan Masters and Gopal Ratnam, "The U.S. Presidential Nominating Process," Council on Foreign Relations, modified February 9, 2016, www.cfr.org/backgrounder/us-presidential-nominating-process.

3. Robert Longley, "Political Party Conventions Day-by-Day," Thought-Co., modified Decmber 4, 2018, www.thoughtco.com/political-party-conventions-day-by-day-3322057.

4. Tia Ghose, "Election Day 2016: How Are Votes Counted?," Live-Science, November 8, 2016, www.livescience.com/56787-how-are-votes-counted.html.

5. Ghose, "Election Day 2016."

Chapter Two: Political Advertising in America

1. "Elections from 1789 to 1828," Virginia Museum of History & Culture, accessed December 17, 2019, www.virginiahistory.org/collections-and-resources/virginia-history-explorer/getting-message-out-presidential-campaign-0.

2. Quoted in Ernest B. Furgurson, "Moment of Truth: Scandal in the Election of 1884," HistoryNet, accessed December 18, 2019, www.historynet.com/moment-of-truth-the-election-of-1884.htm.

3. Kathryn Cramer Brownell, "This Is How Presidential Ads First Got on TV," *TIME*, August 30, 2016, time.com/4471657/political-tv-ads-history.

4. "Running for President," PBS, accessed December 18, 2019, www.pbs.org/wgbh/americanexperience/features/presidents.

5. Mark Green, *Selling Out: How Big Corporate Money Buys Elections, Rams Through Legislation, and Betrays Our Democracy* (New York, NY: HarperCollins, 2002), p. 105.

6. "Special Notices on Political Ads and Solicitations," Federal Elections Commission, 2006, transition.fec.gov/pages/brochures/spec_notice_brochure.pdf.

7. "About 6 in 10 Young Adults in U.S. Primarily Use Online Streaming to Watch TV," Pew Research Center, September 13, 2017, www.pewresearch.org/fact-tank/2017/09/13/about-6-in-10-young-adults-in-u-s-primarily-use-online-streaming-to-watch-tv.

8. Emily Stewart, "Why Everybody Is Freaking Out About Political Ads on Facebook and Google," Vox, November 27, 2019, www.vox.com/recode/2019/11/27/20977988/google-facebook-political-ads-targeting-twitter-disinformation.

9. Stewart, "Why Everybody Is Freaking Out."

10. Stewart, "Why Everybody Is Freaking Out."

11. Julian Sanchez, "Paid Political Ads Are Not the Problem. Our Perceptions Are," *Wired*, November 4, 2019, www.wired.com/story/leave-paid-political-ads-alone.

Chapter Three: Public Image and Voter Perception

1. Kire Sharlamanov and Aleksandar Jovanoski, "The Role of Image in the Political Campaigns," *International Journal of Scientific & Engineering Research 5*, no. 6 (June 2014): p. 603, www.ijser.org/researchpaper/The-Role-of-Image-in-the-Political-Campaigns.pdf.

2. Yilang Peng, "Same Candidates, Different Faces: Uncovering Media Bias in Visual Portrayals of Presidential Candidates with Computer Vision," *Oxford Journal of Communication* 68, no. 12

(October 2018): p. 1, www.researchgate.net/publication/328005872_
Same_Candidates_Different_Faces_Uncovering_Media_Bias_in_
Visual_Portrayals_of_Presidential_Candidates_with_Computer_
Vision.

3. Quoted in Sarah Vowell, *The Partly Cloudy Patriot* (New York, NY: Simon & Schuster, 2002), p. 48.

4. Vowell, *The Partly Cloudy Patriot*, pp. 56–57.

5. Vowell, *The Partly Cloudy Patriot*, p. 57.

Chapter Four: The Fight Against Corruption

1. Quoted in Aaron Rupar, "Trump's Latest Make-Believe About Voter Fraud: Dems Change Shirts and Vote Twice," Vox, November 14, 2018, www.vox.com/2018/11/14/18095592/trump-voter-fraud-disguises-cars-daily-caller-interview.

2. "Debunking the Voter Fraud Myth," Brennan Center for Justice, January 31, 2017, www.brennancenter.org/analysis/debunking-voter-fraud-myth.

3. "Oppose Voter ID Legislation—Fact Sheet," ACLU, accessed December 23, 2019, www.aclu.org/other/oppose-voter-id-legislation-fact-sheet.

4. Quoted in Terry Gross, "Republican Voter Suppression Efforts Are Targeting Minorities, Journalist Says," NPR, October 23, 2018, www.npr.org/2018/10/23/659784277/republican-voter-suppression-efforts-are-targeting-minorities-journalist-says.

Chapter Five: The Future of Campaigning in America

1. Manuela Tobias, "Comparing Facebook Data Use by Obama, Cambridge Analytica," Politifact, March 22, 2018, www.politifact.com/truth-o-meter/statements/2018/mar/22/meghan-mccain/comparing-facebook-data-use-obama-cambridge-analyt.

FOR MORE INFORMATION

Books: Nonfiction

Donovan, Sandra. *Special Interests: From Lobbyists to Campaign Funding.* Minneapolis, MN: Lerner Publications Company, 2016.

Edwards, Sue Bradford. *Electoral College Series: Debating the Issues.* New York, NY: AV2 by Weigl, 2019.

Finne, Stephanie. *How Political Parties Work.* Minneapolis, MN: Core Library, 2015.

Gunderson, Jessica. *Understanding Your Role in Elections.* North Mankato, MN: Capstone Press, 2018.

Books: Fiction

Gutman, Dan. *The Kid Who Became President.* New York, NY: Scholastic, 2012.

Wiles, Deborah. *Revolution.* New York, NY: Scholastic, 2014.

Websites

BrainPOP: Voting
www.brainpop.com/socialstudies/usgovernment/voting
Through videos, quizzes, games, and more, this interactive website teaches users all about voting as well as what it takes to run a successful campaign.

Media Bias/Fact Check
mediabiasfactcheck.com
This independent, nonpartisan website lists thousands of news sources and evaluates them on how biased they are and how accurate their reporting is. For example, an outlet may report all the facts of a story correctly but use certain words to influence whether someone views the story as positive or negative.

Presidential Election Process
www.usa.gov/election
This government website explains how the presidential election process works.

270 to Win
www.270towin.com
This interactive map allows users to make their own election forecasts based on current predictions.

"Why Me? (1988)"
www.youtube.com/watch?v=hdAcX2UEzyA
The FEC made this short video in 1988 to help candidates learn about campaign finance laws. It was posted to YouTube in 2015.

Organizations

American Civil Liberties Union (ACLU)
125 Broad Street, 18th Floor
New York, NY 10004
www.aclu.org
www.instagram.com/aclu_nationwide
twitter.com/aclu
www.youtube.com/aclu
The ACLU has championed for many rights—including voting rights—and its website provides people with useful information on all the issues the organization is fighting for.

HeadCount
104 W 29th Street, 11th Floor
New York, NY 10001
headcount.org
www.instagram.com/HeadCountOrg
twitter.com/HeadCountOrg
People can volunteer with HeadCount to help adults register to vote at concerts. In most cases, volunteers get a free pass to the concert, although HeadCount cautions that they will probably not see the entire concert because they will be working through the opening acts.

Let America Vote
611 Pennsylvania Avenue SE, Suite 143
Washington, DC 20003
www.letamericavote.org/action
twitter.com/letamericavote
This organization advocates for equal voting rights across the United States and encourages people to take advantage of those rights. Its website provides people of all ages with ways to take action within their communities.

Rock the Vote
925 N La Brea Avenue, 4th Floor
Los Angeles, CA 90038
www.rockthevote.org
instagram.com/rockthevote
twitter.com/rockthevote
www.youtube.com/rockthevote
Rock the Vote is a diverse, nonprofit, nonpartisan group that aims
to reach out and empower young voters.

INDEX

PHOTO CREDITS

Cover Cameron Whitman/Shutterstock.com; p. 4 Mark Ralston/AFP via Getty Images; pp. 6, 38, 52, 62, 72 Bettman/Bettmann/Getty Images; p. 8 Miljan Mladenovic/Shutterstock.com; pp. 11, 29 Everett Historical/Shutterstock.com; p. 15 Lucian Perkins/for The Washington Post via Getty Images; p. 16 Susan Schmitz/Shutterstock.com; pp. 20–21 Joseph Sohm/Shutterstock.com; p. 22 Joe Raedle/Getty Images; p. 26 Joe Skipper/Getty Images; p. 28 Win McNamee/Getty Images; p. 31 Leonard Mccombe/The LIFE Picture Collection via Getty Images; p. 32 Yale Joel/Life Magazine/The LIFE Picture Collection via Getty Images; p. 34 Stock Montage/Stock Montage/Getty Images; p. 39 Grey Villet/The LIFE Picture Collection via Getty Images; p. 41 MoveOn.org/Getty Images; p. 46 Stephen Maturen/Getty Images; p. 48 Drew Angerer/Getty Images; p. 55 (left) Saul Loeb/AFP via Getty Images; p. 55 (right) Nicholas Kamm/AFP via Getty Images; p. 64 Frederic J. Brown/AFP via Getty Images; p. 74 J.D. Pooley/Getty Images; p. 78 Michael S. Williamson/The Washington Post via Getty Images; p. 80 Spencer Platt/Getty Images; p. 83 Hill Street Studios/DigitalVision/Getty Images; pp. 86–87 Jeffrey Greenberg/Universal Images Group via Getty Images; p. 89 Mandel Ngan/AFP via Getty Images.

Peter Kogler is a teacher in Buffalo, New York. When he is not teaching or writing, he is collecting lots of old toys and autographs, while also trying to travel and catch up on movies and video games when he can. He wrote this book for his mother, who always talked about not knowing enough about elections, presidents, and their campaigns in America. He hopes that this book will inspire people to get politically involved in their communities and eventually vote in elections that will change the world for the better.